Black Invento

Crafting Over

200 Years of Success

Black Inventors

Crafting Over

200 Years of Success

Keith C. Holmes

For further copies of *Black Inventors, Crafting Over 200 years of Success*

Call: 646-610-1485 or send a check or money order in the amount of: $15.00 (plus shipping and handling). For Canadian and international orders please contact:

Global Black Inventor Research Projects, Inc.
1023 Beverley Road
Brooklyn, New York 11218.

Published by: Global Black Inventor Research Projects, Inc.
Copyright © 2008 by Global Black Inventors Research Projects, Inc.,

ISBN: 978-0979957307

Global Black Inventors Research Projects, Inc.,
1023 Beverley Road
Brooklyn, NY. 11218.
Website: www.globalblackinventor.com
Email: info@globalblackinventor.com or kcholmes50@gmail.com
Facebook: Global Black Inventor Research Projects, Inc.
Twitter: Globalblkinvtr
Linkedin: Keith Holmes

Acknowledgements

This is a perspective that Black people, globally have shared with one another throughout the ages. What we want or need to achieve in life, coupled with hard work leads to success in the long run.

Millions of Black men and women exert a great deal of life-energy, time and resources every day to ensure the success of their loved ones, friends and people both inside and outside of their communities.

This is the same formula of success that our ancestors and forefathers laid for future generations. It is on their shoulders that we stand and rest our heavy burdens. That ageless wisdom and legacy that they have passed on from generation to generation reminds us that we are not working alone on our tasks in life. We have unlimited resources and access to spiritual power to guarantee our success in any chosen endeavor.

I want to thank the many organizations and people that supported my efforts in writing this book. I first thank God for providing me with everlasting peace. When I first explored the idea of writing books about Black inventors, the resources were scarce. The project required lots of leg work, library visits, verification of data, manual entry of data into the computer and long hours spent working into the night. God is good because, for the most part, the resources for an undertaking of this scope are now available online.

I want to express my deepest gratitude to Henry E. Baker and his descendants for making his original research available to the public.

Special thanks to following organizations and people:

The United States Patent Office Repository, New York, for the printed material on United States Patents and Trademarks.

The Schomburg Research Library, New York, NY, and the Howard University Spingarn-Moorland Libraries, Washington, DC, for making Mr. Baker's research materials available. Henry E. Baker's books and research form the backbone of many books written about Black inventors.

My database and web administrator; Kamau Blount, born in Brooklyn, New York, for generously setting up and organizing the data for this project.

Benoit Bofia, born in Dschang, Cameroon for his translation of French written documents into English.

Thomas B. Feaster, born in Miami, Florida and graphic artist who works with Graphika Group, Inc., for his keen artistic skills in capturing the essence of this book. The cover design features the images of Dr. George Washington Carver and Marjorie Stewart Joyner, two very distinguished and prominent African American inventors.

Roslyn Morrison who was raised in Utica, Mississippi, Sandra Lewis, born in St. Ann, Jamaica, and Edwina DeGrant born and raised in Ladysmith, Natal Province, currently KwaZulu, South Africa for all of their editorial support and their insightful comments.

Andrea Tingling, born in London, the United Kingdom for her editorial and public relations assistance.

Dwight Williams, born in Okinawa, Japan, and owner of Community Link Computers for keeping my computers up and running.

I also give thanks and appreciation to our ancestors for leaving a legacy of oral traditions, drawings, paintings, books, artifacts, and evidence of their great works in the field of invention.

I extend my deepest gratitude to my spiritual advisor and mentor, Ra Un Nefer Amen, for the suggestion to write this book. With his guidance, writing a book that sheds light on the innovations, inventions, trademarks and patents of Black people was well worth all of the long hours of research that led to my achieving this goal.

Special thanks to my family for all of their love and support over the years.

The following books provided a wealth of information, and I highly recommend your reading and including them in your library:

Bunmi Adebayo, *Dictionary of African Names, Volume I., Meanings, Pronunciations and Origin*, Authorhouse, 2005.

Henry E. Baker, *The Colored Inventor: A Record of Fifty Years*, New York: Crisis Publishing Company, 1913.

Bill Becoat, *Dream Peddler: The Story of an Entrepreneur*, St. Louis, Mo: Fokl P Power Publishers, 1995.

Louis Haber, *Black Pioneers of Science and Invention*. New York: Harcourt, Brace & World, 1970.

Portia P. James, *The Real McCoy African-American Invention and Innovation*, 1619-1930, Washington, D.C., Anacostia Museum of the Smithsonian Institution, 1989.

Burt McKinley, Jr., *Black Inventor of America*. Portland, Oregon: National Book Company, 1989.

Virginia Ott and Gloria Swanson, *Man with a Million Ideas, Fred Jones Genius/Inventor*, Lerner Publication Company, Minneapolis, Minnesota, 1977.

Walter Rodney, *How Europe Underdeveloped Africa*, Bogle-L'Overture Publications, London and Tanzanian Publishing House, Dar es Salaam, Tanzania

Vivian Sammons, *Black in Science and Medicine*, New York, Hemisphere Publishing Company, 1990.

Patricia Carter Sluby, *The Inventive Spirit of African Americans, Patented Ingenuity*, Westport, Connecticut, Praeger Publishers, 2004.

Morris Turner III, America's *Black Towns and Settlements, A Historical Reference Guide, Volume I.* Missing Pages Production, Rohnert Park, California, 1998.

Juliet E. K. Walker, *The History of Black Business in America: Capitalism, Race Entrepreneurship*, Twayne Publishers, 1998.

Wini Warren, *Black Women Scientists in the United States*, Indiana University Press, Bloomington, Indiana, 1999.

Raymond B. Webster, *African American Firsts in Science and Technology*, Gale Group, Detroit, Michigan, 1999.

Carter G. Woodson, and Charles H. Wesley, *Negro Makers of History 5th Edition Revised*, Washington, D.C., The Associated Publishers, Inc. 1958.

The following websites were an extraordinary resource in finding and compiling information:
African Intellectual Property Organization (OAPI): http://www.oapi.wipo.net,

African Regional Intellectual Property Organization (ARIPO): http://www.aripo.org,

AfriGeneas African Ancestored Genealogy: Website: http://www.afrigeneas.com,

Ancestry website: Website: http://www.ancestry.com,

City Data website: Website: http://www.city-data.com,

Caribbean Icons in Science, Technology & Innovation: Website: http://www.caribbean-icons.org/,

Google Patents website: Website: http://www.google.com/patents,

Trinidad and Tobago Icons in Science and Technology Volume 1 Website: http://www.niherst.gov.tt/s-and-t/awards/tt-icons-vol-1.htm,

UK Intellectual Property Office website: http://gb.espacenet.com,

US Black Engineer and Information Technology Magazine:

Website: http://www.blackengineer.com,

United States Patent and Trademark Office (USPTO): Website: http://www.uspto.gov.

Contents

Tables

Figures

Maps courtesy of www.bjdesign.com

Introduction
Author begins his research in 1988

In 1988, with some very good advice on this matter I decided to resume Henry E. Baker's research on African American innovators and inventors. In January of 2007, a floodgate of information on Black inventors swung open. Google, through its internet service, provided access to the United States Patents Office information, including design patents. I thank God, for the opening of the way. To date, I have managed to find over twelve thousand discoveries, inventions and trademarks by Black inventors from the African Diaspora. As a people of African descent, we may live in Africa, Central and South America, Australia, Canada, the Caribbean, Europe, Russia, the South Pacific, the United Kingdom, and the United States, but as a race, our cultural and ancestral birthplace is the Motherland Africa, the birthplace of our great ancestors and ancient African civilizations. It is important for every Black adult and child to grasp the idea that we as a people have made important and significant discoveries, innovations and inventions. This book will prove that without the inventors, innovators, designers and laborers of African descent, in Africa as well as throughout the African Diaspora, western technology, as we know it today, would not exist.

This book has three parts. The first part explores the role that ancient African civilizations have played in the development of inventions and technologies of today. Part Two, identifies a wealth of inventors who originated in Africa. Part Three explores Black inventors' geographical locations throughout the world.

Henry E. Baker, the Father of Black Inventor Research

In 1900, Henry E. Baker, an African American Patent Examiner in the United States, through his research, found over one thousand patents filed by Black men and women. By 1940, that number had increased, by some conservative estimates, to at least four thousand inventions.

Henry E. Baker was born shortly before the Civil War in Columbus, Mississippi. Baker attended public school in Columbus and later gained admission to Columbus Union Academy. In 1875, Henry E. Baker was admitted to the Naval Academy as cadet midshipman and attended that institution for two years.

In 1877, Baker became a *"copyist"* for the United States Patent Office. Henry E. Baker was promoted to the position of Assistant Patent Examiner. After years of working in that capacity, Mr. Baker decided to explore the history of Black inventors. He was the first person to openly research inventions by Black people. Inventions however, are not classified by race so this made his study a nearly impossible task. Nonetheless, Baker was determined to find this information. He sent out two thousand five hundred letters to patent attorneys and law offices. Some of the responses ridiculed the idea of Black people inventing anything; some patent attorneys responded that they had never heard of a "colored inventor". Baker, however eventually received enough correspondences to document over one thousand inventions by Black men and women.

Early Innovators and Inventors

Name of inventor	Number of patents and Innovations	Location
Benjamin Banneker	One innovative clock design	Ellicott, MD
Andrew J Beard	Seven patents	Eastlake, AL.
Henry Blair	Two patents	Glen Ross, MD.
Henry Creamer	Eight patents	New York, NY.
Shelby J. Davidson	One patent	Fayette, KY.
Joseph H. Dickinson	Forty patents	Detroit, MI.
William Douglass	Eight patents	Erie, PA.
James Doyle	Three patents	Pittsburgh, PA.
Frank J. Ferrell	Fourteen patents	New York, NY.
James Forten	unable to locate the patent	Philadelphia, PA.
Elijah McCoy	Over forty-seven patents	Colchester, Ontario, Canada
Benjamin F. Jackson	Twelve patents	Boston, MA.
William A. Lavalette	One patent	Philadelphia, PA.
Jan E. Matzeliger	Six patents	Paramaribo, Suriname
George W. Murray	Fourteen patents	Rempert, SC.
William B. Purvis	Twenty patents	Philadelphia, PA.
Charles V. Richey	Fourteen patents	Washington, DC.
Granville T. & Lyates Woods	Over forty-eight patents	Cincinnati, OH.

Table 1:   Early Black Innovators and inventors

These inventors alone are credited with over two hundred and forty inventions.

Where do Black inventors come from? Baker's research uncovered Black inventors from Canada, the Caribbean, South America and the United States. History is deeply indebted to Henry E. Baker for his research, insight and courage in pursuing and documenting information about Black inventors and their inventions.

[15]

Part One

Role of Ancient African civilizations in the Development of Today's Inventions and Technologies

Inventiveness and Creativity are Inherent in all Races

Definition of the word invention:

The word invention derived from [ME (Middle English] *invencioun* from [MF (Middle French) invention from the Latin word invention-; invention, from inventus (past part, of inventire to find) + -ion-, -io ion] 1: an act of finding or finding out :< DISCOVERY (~ of the principle of leverage>2a. : the power to conceive new ideas and relationships : productive imagination : INVENTINESS <old crates and boxes are often more stimulating to a child ~ expensive toys>. Furthermore specif, U.S. patent law : a device or process that is not only novel and useful but reflects creative genius, makes a distinct contribution to and advances science, is recognized by masters of science as such an advance and reveals more than a skill of expert artisans or mechanics in discovering new and useful gadgets or process of wide commercial application (Merriam) It also means to originate or create as a product of one's own ingenuity, experimentation and to produce or create with the imagination.

The word patent [ME (Middle English) fr. AF., fr. MF (Middle French) (in letters patents letter patent, fe. of patent adj.] 1. An official document: esp.: one issued by a sovereign power conferring a right or privilege. 2 a: (Philip Babcock Gove)

The invention process did not originate in Europe. It began in one of the oldest known civilizations of the world – Egypt or ancient Kamit. Inventions were introduced by the original inhabitants of Kamit who by all accounts, drawings, statues and scrolls, were black. Many of today's inventions have their roots in the ancient civilizations of Kamit, Mesopotamia, Sumer, and Indus Kush. The inventions from these ancient civilizations were transferred to sub-Saharan Africa, and indeed, to the rest of the world. There was a working relationship between Blacks, north and south of the Sahara desert. Although many inventions are particularly listed as having originated in Egypt, they were likely developed by Africans beyond the borders of ancient Egypt. The following list of inventions is from the *Ancient Egyptian Materials and Industries* by A. Lucas and J.R. Harris. The countless paintings, statues, and figurines from ancient Egypt, depict brown and black people with African features that clearly resemble those of Black people in the Diaspora. The following list of ancient Egyptian innovations and inventions is by no means exhaustive, but it provides an idea of the link between today's industries and the inventions of ancient Egypt or Kamit.

[17]

Ancient Egypt's Innovations and Inventions	Products used to make inventions
Adhesives	albumins, beeswax, clay, gelatin, glue, gum, gypsum, natron, resin, solder, starch, salt, miscellaneous, and unidentified adhesives)
Agriculture	almonds, barley, dates, figs, garlic, ginger, grapes, lentils, lettuce, maize, millet, olives, onions, palm, sorghum...etc.
Alcoholic Beverages	beer and brewing: wine and wine making: distilled spirits), malts, sugar
Animal Products:	bone, butter, cheese, feathers, gut, hair, horn, ivory, leather, mother of pearl, ostrich eggshell, parchment, tortoise-shell, marine and fresh water shells
Animal Husbandry	camels, cattle, goats, horses, ducks, chickens
Bee keeping	beeswax, honey
Basketry	coiled basketry, twined work, matting work
Beverages and Wine	grape, dates, palm
Building Materials	asphalt, brick and brick making, cement, gypsum, stone, mortar, plaster, sun-dried brick, wood
Clay	bricks, mortar, plaster, pottery
Cosmetics	perfumes, essential oils, incense, cleansing cream
Dyes	Egyptian blue (indigo), black, brown, green, purple, red, yellow
Embalming & Funerary Rites	rituals and ceremonies to bury the dead properly, mummification
Fibers	basketry, brushes, cordage, matting, papyrus, woven, fabrics, spinning, addition, weaving linen and other materials
Glazed Ware	glazed steatite, faience variants, glazed quartz, glazed pottery, glazing methods and media, kilns
Gums and Resins	acacia, cedar, copal, frankincense, myrrh, pine
Ink	pigment: black, brown, green, blue, grey, orange, red, white, yellow
Metals and Alloys	alumina, aluminum, antimony, brass, cobalt, copper, copper-antimony alloy, copper gold-alloy, copper-lead alloy, bronze and bronze-lead alloys, gold and electrum, hematite, iron, iron-copper alloy, lead, lead-copper alloy, lead-tin alloy, platinum, silver, tin
Minerals	alum, barites, cobalt, compounds, emery, feldspar, graphite, manganese compounds, mica, natron, nitre, salt and sulfur
Mineral Spirits	turpentine, alcohol

Oils, Fats and Waxes	almond oil, belanos oil, bean oil, castor oil, cedar oil, coconut oil, colocynth oil, croton oil, frankincense, juniper oil, lettuce oil, lilies oil, linseed oil, malabathrum oil, myrrh, olive, palm, radish oil, safflower, sesame oil, walnut oil
Paints and Pigments	black, blue, brown, green, grey, orange, pink, red, white, yellow
Plants	cattails, juniper berries, palms
Precious and Semi-Precious Stones	diamonds, emeralds, gold, opal, ruby, silver…etc.
Pottery and Pottery Making	kilns, moulds, varnished, glazed, polishing,
Spices	cinnamon, dill, cumin, parsley, onions…etc.
Stones	other building stones and precious stones, stone vessels, granite, limestone, sandstone.
Textiles	cotton cloth
Tools	chisels, brushes, dowels, hinges, nails, axes, plows
Wood	foreign timber: Egyptian timber, beech wood, birch, carob-wood, cypresswood ebony, elm, fig, hornbeams, lime wood, maple woodworking, bark silicified wood, charcoal, plywood

Table 2:   Ancient Egyptian Innovations and Inventions (from Ancient Egyptian Materials and Industries by A. Lucas and J.R. Harris)

Africans develop their own Innovations and Inventions

Below is a list of industries, crafts and traditions developed in Africa, prior to the arrival of Europeans.

Agriculture	cultivating grasses into grain crops kram-kram, maize, millet (finger, pearl, shama, guinea), sorghum, tef, terracing, irrigation: African rice, emmer, Ethiopian oats, fonio, irregular barley
Animal Husbandry	camel, cattle, donkeys, goats, horses, mules
Animal Products	milk, meat, fish, fresh and dried fish, animal hides, leather, ivory
Architecture and Building	bricks, sinking well shafts, earthwork systems, houses, irrigation systems, buildings
Beverages	coffee, kola, sorrel, sorghum beer, millet beer
Ceramics	pots, plates, bowls
Ceremonies, Religion, Rituals	development of priests and priestesses, initiation systems for transforming boys and girls into men and women, naming and marriage ceremonies, strengthening spiritual ties with God and our ancestors, knowledge of the Supreme Being
Dyes	indigo, cam wood, kola nuts, redwood tree, tie-dye,

	resist dye. Kuntunkuni bark, mud
Fibers	baskets, string instruments, cordage, furniture, mats, hats, nets, shields, straps, tools, furniture, musical instruments, drinking straws
Food	over 2,000 plants have been identified as food sources in Africa. African eggplant, African yam bean, anchote, avocado, baobab, breadfruit, cashew fruit, cizaki, coconut, guinea yam, potato yam, other yams, bananas, bush beans, Ethiopian mustard, cashews, cola, cow peas, ground nuts, okra, guava, hausa yams, mango, papaya, pitanga cherry, plantain, pomegranate, Sudan potato, sweet potato, Livingstone potato, wing bean roots, ginger, tiger nut, sabah nut, vigna roots, bananas, watermelon, melon, gourds...etc.
Funerary Rites	rituals and ceremonies to bury the dead properly
Kingship, Queen Mothership	development of kings, queen mothers, chiefs
Language	over 2,000 languages in Africa
Mining, Precious gems, Minerals and Metals:	copper, diamonds, gold, iron, metal smiths silver, tin, uranium...etc.
Oil	palm butter, palm oil, shea butter, olive
Other	coffee, cotton, dyes, gum, ivory, leather, palm, pepper, groundnut
Textiles	tailors, looms, weavers, cotton, cloth, leather, animal, hides furs, feathers, (sandals, leather jackets, leather pouches...etc), cloth made from cotton, tree bark, jute, flax, raffia palm, batik, tie-dye, resist, kente cloth, kikoi cloth, mud cloth, silk, dyes made from minerals and vegetables
Tools	axe, hoe, knives, spears, bows and arrows, nets, traps, snares, blades, harpoon points, arrow points, hammers, hairpins made of copper, iron, ivory and wood
Traditional Medicine and Plants	today 80% of the people in Africa use traditional healers and medicine. South Africa alone has over 24,000 indigenous plants, which represent 10% of the Earth's higher plants. Twenty three African Nations fully recognize the work, practice and service that the Traditional African Healers have been providing to Africans. Thousands of plants used for their curative properties are now recognized and are being patented.
Wood	furniture, masks, ornamental and religious carvings, timber wooden bowls, pots...etc.

Table 3: African developed Innovations and Inventions

[20]

Part Two

Black Inventors' Ancestral Links to Africa

World Leaders in Patents

From the chart below it is clear that there are no African or Caribbean countries ranked in the top twenty-five countries where patents were granted in 1998; however, this chart does not specify the number of Black people who were granted patents in countries outside of Africa or the Caribbean. Black people who live in Australia, Austria, Belgium, Canada, France, Germany, and the Netherlands. Norway, Russia, Sweden, the United Kingdom and the United States, regularly file for and receive patents. According to Nationmaster.com, Americans are 15% more innovative than the Japanese. Even so, the Japanese have 3.5 times more patents (**NationMaster.com, Patents Granted per million people 1998**).

Rank	Country	Description – Patents granted per million people 1998
1.	Japan	994 per million people
2.	Korea, South	779 per million people
3.	United States	289 per million people
4.	Sweden	271 per million people
5.	Germany	235 per million people
6.	France	205 per million people
7.	Luxembourg	202 per million people
8.	Netherlands	189 per million people
9.	Finland	187 per million people
10.	Switzerland	183 per million people
11.	Austria	165 per million people
12.	Russia	131 per million people
13.	Ireland	106 per million people
14.	Slovenia	105 per million people
15.	New Zealand	103 per million people
16.	Norway	103 per million people
17.	Ukraine	84 per million people
18.	United Kingdom	82 per million people
19.	Australia	75 per million people
20.	Israel	74 per million people
21.	Belgium	72 per million people
22.	Latvia	71 per million people
23.	Romania	71 per million people
24.	Georgia	67 per million people
25.	Mongolia	56 per million people

Table 4:   Patents granted by country (Top 25), 1998

This book will list some of the patents granted to Black people living in predominately White countries, and the patents granted to Blacks living in predominately Black countries. However, the new giants in the world of patents and invention will be China and India, given the enormous size of their populations and their rapid use of technology. Both countries have their own patent offices and have already granted millions of patents to their citizens. Japan and South Korea also have their own patent offices and have also granted millions of patents to their citizens. But the new millennium promises to usher in a tidal wave of new inventions from African, Caribbean, Central and South American countries. Countries such as Argentina, Brazil, Ethiopia, Ghana, Jamaica, Kenya, Mexico, Nigeria, South Africa, Trinidad and Tobago, Uganda and Zimbabwe are paving the way for a number of new inventions each year.

It is important to note that Africans were inventors long before Europeans started to document and assign patents for people's ideas and inventions.

"Apart from inventiveness, we must also consider the borrowing of technology. When a society for whatever reason finds itself technologically trailing behind others, it catches up not so much by independent inventions but by borrowing. Indeed, very few of man's major scientific discoveries have been separately discovered in different places by different people. Once a principle or tool is known, it spreads or diffuses to other people. Why then did European technology fail to make its way into Africa during the many centuries of contact between the two continents? The basic reason is that the very nature of Afro-European trade was highly unfavorable to the movement of positive ideas and techniques from the European capitalist system to the African pre-capitalist (communal, feudal and pre-feudal system of production). (Rodney, Technical Stagnation and Distortion of the African Economy in the Pre-Colonial Epoch)

Why then did European technology fail to make its way into Africa during the many centuries of contact between the two continents? The answer to this is that Europeans did not readily exchange ideas or innovative technologies with African people.

In the Congo, the slave trade did not get under way without grave doubts and opposition from the king of the state of Kongo at the beginning of the sixteenth century. He asked for masons, priests, clerks, physicians; but instead he was overwhelmed by slave ships sent from Portugal, and a vicious trade was opened up by playing off one part of the Kongo kingdom against another. The king of the Kongo had conceived of possibilities of mutually beneficial interchange between his people and the European state, but the latter forced him to specialize in the export of human cargo. *(Rodney, How Europe Became the Dominant Section of a World-Wide Trade System)*

[23]

Census Classification Systems Used to Identify Black people

One of the most profound findings in researching information about people of color and their inventions was the classification system devised to accurately document information about Black people. This system was used as a decoy to keep Black people from identifying one another as members of the same race. It was common practice to classify Black people under a host of different categories: Aborigine, African, Afro, Black, Caribbean, Colored, Dravidian, Khaffir, Moors, Mulatto, Native African, Negro, Octoroon, Quadroon, Slave, South African, West Indian (The Generations Network)...etc.

Yet, despite this system of classification, Black people have still used their intelligence and creativity, in spite of tremendous odds to patent their ideas and inventions. In some cases, they kept their original names. For example, Santie Sabalala emigrated from South Africa to the United States, and on the 1920 United States Census report, though color of race was reported as Black, his mother and father tongue was identified as "Khaffir".

When one looks at the early census, the two predominant references for White people are Caucasian and White.

Astonishing in this research, is the number of enslaved and free people of color who knew that their birthplace was Africa. You will find in the 1880, 1900, 1910, 1920 and the 1930 United States Census, Black people identifying their place of birth, or their parents' place of birth as Africa. This is an important point. Though forced into slavery and transferred from their homeland, Black people still maintained a connection with their birth or ancestral homeland, Africa - in some cases keeping their names or some of their cultural or religious practices.

In the United States Censuses of 1850 and 1880 there were well over ten thousand Black men and women in the United States who stated they came from such places as: Africa, Central African Republic, West Africa, Ethiopia, and South Africa.

The 1901 Census of England, also clearly states the origination of some of the Black people in England: *Natives of Africa, Ashanti (West Africa), East Africa, South Africa.*

In the 1910 United States Federal Census, a number of Black men and women identified their birthplace as Africa, or their mother's or father's birthplace as Africa.

In the 1920 United States Census, there were both Black and White people showing their birthplace to be: Africa, the Central African Republic, and South Africa. Both black and white people have used the name Africa as part of their last name.

The Military records of United States Civil War soldiers (1861-1865), show the word "Colored" in over two hundred and thirty eight thousand cases for both the Confederate and Union Armies. The same term "Colored" appears in reference to American Civil War soldiers for over one hundred and eighty nine thousand men who fought in the Union army as U.S. Colored Troops.

During World War I (1917-1918), one of the terms used on the United States Draft Registration Card was "African". It was used to describe the over three hundred thousand Black men whose draft registration cards bore that classification. The term "Black" appeared on over one million World War I Draft Registration Cards (1917-1918).

Throughout World War II (1938-1945), one of the terms used by the United States World War II Army Enlistment Records was "Negro". It appeared on over seven hundred records. The term "Negro" was also used to describe the over two hundred fifty thousand black men whose draft registration cards bore that classification.

For the duration of the Korean War (1950-1957), one of the terms used on the United States Draft Registration Card to describe the over sixteen thousand Black men who were causalities of the Korean War was "Negro".

[25]

Worth mentioning in this book is the common thread that linked Black people during the 1800's and 1900's, whether they were born in Austria, Brazil, Canada, the Caribbean, Central and South America, England, Ireland, France, Germany, India, Italy, the Netherlands, Norway, Poland, Portugal, Russia, Spain, Sweden and Switzerland. Black people had one thing in common; they were immigrating to the United States in significant numbers.

The United States Census records clearly indicate the place of birth, and race of all immigrants. Some Black immigrants filed for patents after they entered the United States while others filed for patents in their native countries before immigrating to the United States.

What has changed from 1913 to the Present?

A number of circumstances have changed, since Henry E. Baker wrote *The Colored Inventor: A Record of Fifty Years* in 1913. For one thing, Jim Crow is dead and voting, legislative and civil rights laws are now in place. Business opportunities for Black people have expanded, globally. The income of African Americans alone exceeds eight hundred billion dollars; worldwide, the income of all Black people amounts to trillions of dollars. In addition, if we factor in the value of gold, diamonds, petroleum and other natural resources that belong to Black people their wealth increases exponentially.

Politically, Black men and women now occupy elected and non-elected positions as heads of states, presidents, prime ministers, government ministers, governors, senators, congressman, mayors and other governmental offices. These positions put the control of hundreds of millions of people and trillions of dollars in natural resources directly under the control of Black men and women. It means that the potential to resolve worldwide political and domestic issues rests in their hands.

Globally, Black people today are in the position of controlling their own countries, cities, land, homes, businesses, religious institutions, and educational institutions. Black people are in a position to control the

[26]

economic resources in their communities in order to improve their physical and spiritual condition. The test of any people is how they transcends the devastating effects of inferior education, disease, drugs, poor nutrition, and lack of a moral compass. For Black people, it will take trust, cooperative economics and spirituality to establish a unified international purpose and the restoration of the principles of ancient African civilizations.

The former African and Caribbean colonies of Europe are now independent with the Blacks of South Africa, lifting the yoke of apartheid in 1994, with their first elections. Although the yoke of colonialism is not entirely broken, the combined resources of Africa and the African Diaspora represent a treasure trove of talent, innovations and inventions that could be the deciding factor in leading Black people, and indeed the world, out of misery and into a world of challenges lined with golden opportunities.

Today, African and Caribbean nations face what is called a "brain drain". Those with engineering, scientific and technical skills are emigrating from their countries to seek opportunities in the Americas, Asia, Australia, Canada, Europe, Latin America, the Middle East, Russia, and the United Kingdom. For more information into this subject read. (Mutume)

The same problem is occurring domestically in the United States with many young, Black men and women leaving rural towns and cities to pursue opportunities in large urban areas. In the process, there is a loss of inventiveness, innovation, culture, customs and land, but a number of African Americans are waking up to the idea of owning their own homes and properties as as well gaining economic and political control of their respective towns, cities and counties.

Black people outside of Africa are looking for that common ancestral thread that ties them back to their true heritage. DNA testing, exploring their roots, changing their ideas about Africa and adopting African names are just a part of this process.

Patents are not classified by race; therefore, researching the names of Black inventors from the past and the present is cumbersome. Black

[27]

inventors cannot be traced through their names only. The researcher must have access to reliable information that connects the inventor's name to his or her race. African inventors with traditional African names are easier to identify and categorize as Black inventors. Yet, I might add that there are Black men and women who are inventing and patenting their ideas in their birthplaces. This book identifies some of those ideas and inventions. In the following pages we will continue to explore the broad spectrum of Black innovations and inventions.

Part Three

Black Inventors' Influence Throughout the World

Black Inventors Educated and Trained Globally

Over sixty-eight Historically Black Colleges and Universities (HBCU) exist in the United States, and hundreds more colleges and universities are located in the Caribbean and in Africa. Black students are now free to pursue their educational goals in: Canada, Central and South America, Europe, the United Kingdom, Russia, Asia, the Middle East, the Pacific Rim countries, and indeed throughout the Diaspora. Black students' access to increased higher education opens new doors to ideas, resources and connections that will play an important role in the fields of innovation, invention and trade marking. It will also be the deciding factor in developing new businesses and global economic partnerships. Although opportunities for Black inventors seem to be increasing, there is still a need for a national and international agenda that can pool their ideas and resources, as they continue to seek economic empowerment.

It was clear to Henry E. Baker that Black businessmen, businesswomen and inventors were willing to work together to improve the lives of people inside and outside of their communities. My research shows a continuing effort in that regard.

Henry E. Baker summarized it best when he observed that the progress of Black people and humanity rests on the shoulders of the dream makers, innovators, inventors, men and women who patent, and trademark, their ideas.

Every aspect of inventing and trade marking is aimed at raising capital, creating and building viable businesses, and employing and paying people wages that will help them to accomplish their life goals. Black inventors have achieved that goal by patenting their ideas in agriculture, business, technology, medicine science, and many other fields. Their ideas, labor and inventions have transformed people, nations and continents, and have collectively generated trillions of dollars over the last two hundred years. With optimism, creativity, our ancestral roots, access to natural resources and God's inspiration and guidance, Black inventor's will play a major role in uplifting our people and humanity.

[30]

The Increase in Black Populations Worldwide

Below is a list of countries and regions and the estimated Black populations in those areas (Black Latin America), (Wikipedia Foundations).

Countries and Regions	Estimated number of Black population
Canada and the United States	Over forty million people of African Descent
Mexico	Over one million people of African Descent
Central America	Over six million people of African Descent
South America	Over one hundred million people of African Descent
Caribbean	Over fourteen million people of African descent
Europe	Over three million people of African descent
United Kingdom	Over seven million people of African descent
Africa	Over seven hundred million people of African descent
Middle East	Over four million people of African descent
India	Over two hundred million Black people (Dravidians)
Australia and South Pacific	Over five million people of African Descent.

Table 5: Black populations globally

The numbers combined, amount to over one billion Black people. This number of people alone could account for millions of ideas, discoveries, innovations, inventions, and trademarks.

Earliest Documented Black Inventors

Many enslaved or free Africans suffered a great injustice because although their ideas were patented they never received recognition or monetary compensation for their inventions. Although a cross section of industries benefited financially from these ideas, for the most part the Black inventors and their people did not. Some of the earliest patents filed by Black men and women were filed in Canada, France, Haiti, Jamaica, the United Kingdom and the United States.

In 1909, Aborigine inventor, David Unaipon of Australia, received a patent for an improvement in sheep shears.

African American, Thomas L. Jennings, Richmond, Virginia, granted a United States patent for a dry cleaning, procedure namely dry scouring of clothes on March 3rd, 1821.

Black Canadian, inventor Stephen C. Skanks, Toronto, Canada, awarded a patent for a sleeping car berth register on July 21st, 1897.

Afro-Cuban inventor, Maurico R. Plancht, Havana, Cuba, received a patent for a pneumatic tire on May 29th, 1923.

Black Frenchman, Lucien Maurice, Paris, France, granted a patent for an accumulator of heat on May 30th, 1899.

Ethiopian inventor, Birrou Ayana, London, England, received a patent for a typewriter adapted for use in Ethiopian languages by the use of special signs on August 9th, 1932.

Haitian inventor Miguel Boom, Port Au Prince, Haiti, awarded a patent for a music-box on November. 14th, 1883.

Jamaican inventor, Dugald Clark, St. Thomas in the East, Jamaica, granted a patent for an application of steam to sugar milling in 1769, making him one of the earliest black men to receive a patent in the Western Hemisphere.

Nigerian inventor, Thomas King Ekundayo Phillips, London, England, earned a British patent for improvements in palm oil extracting machines on June 12th, 1913.

South African inventor Santie Sabalala, Cleveland, Ohio, earned a patent for a car brake on May 18th, 1919.

Senegalese inventor Konare Kaw Ousmane, Dakar, Senegal, received a patent for a machine to make bricks of chipboard of all types on January 24th, 1942.

Trinidadian inventor Hubert Julian, Montreal, Canada, granted a patent for an airplane safety appliance, May 9th, 1921.

The preceding list of names, clearly illustrates that the creativity to develop and patent ideas did not exist exclusively in the United States.

Black Inventors From 1769 – 2007

The number of inventions discovered to date; from 1769-1899 by Black inventors unmistakably indicates a steady progression from simple agricultural inventions to more sophisticated and revolutionary inventions. Sparked by that same innate intelligence inherent in every race, Africans, prior to their enslavement, had developed their own languages, religion, agricultural systems, architectural designs, books, education, iron smelting, animal husbandry, identification system of plants for medicinal and commercial use, fishing, hunting, pottery, basketry and leather tanning. Although the majority of enslaved Africans were deployed in agricultural, menial and service tasks on New World plantations, they used certain transferable skills that they had already cultivated in Africa. Carpentry, iron smelting, blacksmithing, jewelry making, weaving, dyeing, pottery making, basketry and the making of musical instruments are all examples of this. Some of the skills developed under enslavement such as carpentry, blacksmithing, pattern making, to name a few – only enhanced the explosion of inventions, which came from African, European and Native American skills and technology.

"...a vast majority of the west-coast nations were far from being "naked savages" living in primitive squalor. Several towns near the west coast were more populous, at the time, than any but the largest European cities. There were kingdoms and commonwealths comparable in size with many European nations, and even the smaller tribes had defined and often complex cultures. The West Africans had invented their own forms of architecture and their own methods of weaving. Many of them possessed flocks of donkeys and great herds of cattle, sheep, and goats. They were skilled workers in wood, brass, and iron, which last they had learned to smelt long before the white men came. Many of their communities had highly religions, well-organized economic systems, efficient agricultural practices, and admirable codes of law. We have only in recent years begun to appreciate. West Africa's contribution to sculpture, folk, literature and music". (Mannix)

We have to appreciate the inventions by Africans before, during and after the advent of slavery.

Between 1700-1899 an explosion of prolific and profound Black inventors changed the course of history in the United States. The twentieth century saw a complete change in the energy sources of developed nations – from physical power to electric power and from petroleum to atomic energy. Now we are experiencing the development of alternative, environmentally friendly energy sources known as green energy.

[34]

According to my research, from 1900-1999, Black inventors patented over 6,000 inventions. Over time, the number of inventions by Black inventors increased exponentially. From 2000-2007, Blacks patented over 5,000 inventions. Bear in mind that these numbers are subject to change as new inventions by Black inventors are constantly being uncovered. These patents mean that Black men and women were inventing, filing for patents, selling their patents and setting up businesses. The numbers of patents reflect a fraction of actual inventions by Black people. As matter of fact, if one includes all of the ideas, innovations and discoveries that Black men and women were responsible for on a worldwide scale, these inventions would number in the millions.

Although some things have changed, there are still vast numbers of people in the world who are unaware of the local and global innovative accomplishments of Black people. The next few pages will give you an idea of some of the early inventions as well as those countries where Black inventors reside. The lists are diverse, and span the entire globe. The inventions themselves range from simple designs to the technologically complex. Some of the inventions represent the earliest inventions found thus far.

The World

Figure 1 Map of the World

[35]

List of Early Black Inventors throughout the World, Organized by State/Country

Inventor	Invention	Date of Patent	City, State or Country
Powell Johnson	Eye protector	Nov. 02,1880	Barton, Alabama
JoAnn Geer	Double bladed windshield wiper with a central sponge portion	Feb. 04, 2003	Anchorage, Alaska
Henry O. Flipper	Tent	Dec. 06, 1898	Nogales, Arizona
James Henry Smith,	Weather-board gage	May 31, 1887	Little Rock, Arkansas
Anthony K. Quansah,	Compartment containers	Jan. 06, 1998	Australia
Kwaku Frimpong Ansah, et al.	Method of and system for transcribing dictations in text files and for revising the text	May 01, 2003	Vienna, Austria
Reginald L. Gooding,	Process for treating steel to prevent rusting	Apr. 14, 1916	Bridgetown, Barbados
Billo Diallo, et al.	Taxane and taxine derivatives from penecillium S	Sep. 29, 1998	Brussels, Belgium
Edward E. August,	Rail joint	Dec. 18, 1923	British Honduras (Belize)
Reine M Zouliat	Device for indoor security	Dec. 20, 2001	Cotonou, Benin
Joseph Chuma, et al	Microwave filter	Feb. 22, 2001	Gaborone, Botswana
John H P Ibbott	Key	Aug. 14,1906	New Amsterdam, British Guiana
Alexander P. Ashborne	Process for preparing coconut for domestic use	Jun. 01, 1875	Oakland, California
Thomas Njimi	Method for preparing desmosterol	Apr. 09, 1974	Yaounde, Cameroon
Stephen C. Skanks	Sleeping car berth register	Jul. 21, 1897	Toronto, Canada
Cesaire Sokambi	Crank-geared manioc	Dec. 20, 2000	Central African Republic
Gueti Guindja	Enriched "nigue-flour"	Mar. 12,1997	N"damena, Chad
E.N. Onwuka, et al.	Hierarchy mobile packet communication network and its communication method	Mar. 03,2004	Beijing, China
Olobo J. Obaje, et al.	Trans-acidolysis process for the preparation of carbohydrate fatty-acid esters	Jan. 08, 2004	Singapore, China
Willis H. West	Window ventilator	Dec. 19, 1916	Trinidad, Colorado
Anlamvo Nguie	Processing yam into flour	Jan. 16, 1989	Brazzaville, Congo
Sarah Boone	Ironing Board	Apr. 26, 1892	New Haven, Connecticut
Ali Kone	Vitreous materials with ionic conductivity, the preparation of same and the electrochemical applications thereof	Apr. 23, 1985	Cote D'Ivoire, Ivory Coast
Maurico R. Plancht	Pneumatic tube	May 29, 1923	Havana, Cuba
Jacob M. Henriquez	Shaving brush	Jun. 25, 1901	Curacao, West Indies
George M. Williams	Corn Planter	Feb. 17, 1885	Newark, Delaware
Sanya Olufemi	Method for the sorting program locations	Oct. 18, 1994	Villigen, Denmark

[36]

List Early Black Inventors throughout the World, Organized by State/Country

Inventor	Invention	Date of Patent	City, State or Country
Landrow Bell	Locomotive smoke stack	May 23, 1871	Washington, DC.
Guillermo Solomon	Automobile parking device	Nov. 14, 1939	Santiago, Dominican Republic
Azieb Afeworki	Hair roller with elliptical cross section	Apr. 23, 2002	Eritrea
Akililu Lemma, et al.	Method of producing a molluscicide from endod	May 26, 1974	Addis Ababa, Ethiopia
James Henry Haines	Portable shampooing-basin	Sep. 28, 1897	Tampa, Florida
Maurice Lucien	Accumulator of heat	May 30, 1899	Paris, France
Tramline Mado	Creame Sagina	Mar. 15, 1985	Libreville, Gabon
James M. Brooks	Improvement in cotton planter	Feb. 11, 1873	Woodbury, Georgia
Gerard Georges, et al.	Quick insertion arrangement especially for sparkplugs in combustion engines	Jul. 24, 1973	Wolfsburg, Germany
John A. Boah	Temperature gradient zone melting utilizing infrared radiation	Jan. 04, 1977	Kumasi, Ghana
Nema Mathieu Kolie	Smoke-house appliance for food products	Jan. 1996	Conakry, Guinea
Cyriaque Kouadio	Method for surface shading using stored texture map	May 2, 2002	Honolulu, Hawaii
Kwesi E. Abraham, et al.	Method for surface shading using stored texture	May 23, 1995	Boise, Idaho
Elijah Smith	Windmill	Sep. 17, 1878	Good Hope, Illinois
William H. Jackson	Switch	Mar. 09, 1897	Indianapolis, Indiana
John W. West	Running gear	Oct. 18, 1870	Sayorville, Iowa
Mathias Christian Zohoungbogbo	Pharmaceutical composition for treating side-effects of a diet with reduced amount of carbohydrates	Dec. 22, 1999	Torino, Italy
Kone Dossungui et al.	Method for extracting manioc (cassava) pulp, by wet means, particularly for preparing manioc (cassava) flour or meal and device implement	Jun. 20, 1986	Cote D'Ivoire, Ivory Coast
Euston E. Black	Pen-extractor	Jul. 05, 1921	Alligator Pond, Jamaica
William Amaah-Ofosu, et al.	Snubber energy recovery circuit for protecting switching devices from voltage and current	Aug. 22, 1995	Kawasaki, Japan
William S. Pittman	Spark-arrester	Jan. 03, 1893	Pierceville, Kansas
James R. Mock	Muzzle-loading firearm	May 31, 1859	Elizabethtown, Kentucky
John Kilolo Mangeli	Method for making detergent compositions	Dec. 16, 1975	Kalama Location, Kenya
Mabahle Makhaya	Curtain rail accessory	Jun. 19, 1997	Maseru, Lesotho
Norbert Rillieux	Evaporating pan	Aug. 26, 1843	New Orleans, Louisiana

List Early Black Inventors throughout the World, Organized by State/Country

Inventor	Invention	Date of Patent	City, State or Country
Albert R Ratsimamanga et al.	Sodium oxamate for the treatment of diabetic conditions	Oct. 09, 2001	Antananarivo, Madagascar
Robert B. Lewis	Machine cleaning and drying feathers	Jun. 27, 1840	Hallowell, Maine
Maluwa Behringer, et al.	Improved low temperature cooking cereal-based food products	Aug. 20, 2001	Malawi
Salime Sylla, et al.	Monomers derived from pre-halogenated sultones and polymers obtained from these monomers	May 9, 1995	Bamako, Mali
Henry Blair	Cotton planter	Aug. 31, 1836	Melross, Maryland
William F. McCarty	Improvement in flat-irons	Jan. 21, 1879	Boston, Massachusetts
Jerome Carcasse, et al.	Machine which produces inexhaustible electrical energy	Sep. 13, 1991	Curepipe, Mauritania
Lawrence H. Knox	2a-substituted methyl androstanes	Sep. 19, 1961	Mexico City, Mexico
Turner Byrd Jr.	Improvement in holders for reins for horses	Feb. 06, 1872	Williamsville, Michigan
Alexander Miles	Hair tonic	Dec. 11, 1883	Duluth, Minnesota
Benjamin H. Taylor	Rotary engine	Apr. 23, 1878	Rosedale, Mississippi
Michael C. Harney	Lantern or lamp	Aug. 19, 1884	St. Louis, Missouri
William D. Davis	Riding saddle	Oct. 06, 1896	Fort Assiniboine, Montana
William S. Campbell	Self-setting animal trap	Aug. 30, 1881	Columbus, Nebraska
Gebre Admasu, et al.	Vehicle guidance system	Jun. 30, 1992	Amersfoort, Netherlands
Chuko H Ejiofor, et al.	Specific and reversible carbon monoxide sensor	Apr. 12, 1994	Las Vegas, Nevada
Brainerd T. Olcott	Shield for the knees of trousers	May 11, 1886	Keene, New Hampshire
Joseph R. Hawkins	Improved gridiron	Mar. 26, 1845	West Windsor, New Jersey
Richard Bowie Spikes	Billiard cue racks	Oct. 11, 1910	Albuquerque, New Mexico
Ignaz Ramminger	Detacher for detaching horses	Jul. 17, 1860	New York, New York
Boureima Mossi,	Electronic anti-theft device	Nov. 11, 1995	Niamey, Niger
Hardy Spears	Portable shield for infantry	Dec. 27, 1870	Snow Hill, North Carolina
Solomon O. Nwaka	Human elongase genes uses thereof and compounds for modulating same	Jun. 02, 2002	Nova Scotia, Canada

List Early Black Inventors throughout the World, Organized by State/Country

Inventor	Invention	Date of Patent	City, State or Country
William M. Binga	Street sprinkling apparatus	Jul. 22, 1879	Cincinnati, Ohio
Lee R. Chambliss	Vehicle-wheel	May 31, 1898	Langston, Oklahoma
Alexander K. Bonsu et. al.	Apparatus and method for treating sesquisulfate waste streams	Nov. 05, 2002	GreeleyPike, Pennsylvania
Okon Essiet	Process for extracting a sweetening agent from dioscoreophyllum cumminsii berries	Aug. 29, 1972	Portland, Oregon
Jose G. Recuero	Aeroplane	Jul. 16, 1918	Panama City, Panama
Joseph R. Winters	Fire escape ladder	May 07, 1878	Chambersburg, Pennsylvania
Kenneth Ogbonna Udeh, et al.	Method of obtaining beta-1,4-xylanase	Dec. 20, 1999	Poland
Abraham Pugsley,	Blind stop(device for operating blind-slats	Jul. 29, 1890	Jamestown, Rhode Island
Ogigure Dzouzef, et al.	Initial composition for producing white cement clinker	Nov. 23, 1990	Russia
Alton Liston , et al.	System for passing two color television signals through non-linear path	Oct. 10, 1978	St. Thomas, Virgin Islands
Belisario Silfa	Puzzle	Apr. 25, 1905	Santo Domingo
Oluyinka A. Awojobi	Radiation measuring and integrating device	Mar. 09, 1971	Glasgow, Scotland
Yvon R. Dommergues, et al.	Microbiological process for controlling the productivity of cultivated plants	May 22, 1979	Dakar, Senegal
James Gregory	Motor	Apr. 26, 1887	Bogansville, Kentucky
Tesfamariam Yosief, et al.	Cytotoxic alkaloid derivatives including Asmarine A and B isolated from a sponge	Jul. 16, 2002	Tres Contos, Spain
Ahmed A R. Elagib	Hydraulically balanced bridge for measuring temperature differences	Feb. 20, 1968	Khartoum, Sudan
Fedna Stoll	Thermal solar dehydrator	Oct. 05, 1999	Paramaribo, Suriname
Ogbonna, Daniel, et al.	Surgical method	Oct. 28, 1997	Stromstad, Sweden
Anyanwu Nwaeze	Process for determining 17-ketosteroids in urine and blood and solutions for carrying out this process	Jul. 14, 1970	Zurich, Switzerland
Frank S. Mchuma	Bathroom appliances	Jan. 04, 1983	Dar-Es-Salaam, Tanzania
Elbert R. Robinson	Electric railway trolley	Sep. 19, 1893	Nashville, Tennessee
Frank Winn	Direct acting steam engine	Dec. 04, 1888	Dallas, Texas

List Early Black Inventors throughout the World, Organized by State/Country

Inventor	Invention	Date of Patent	City, State or Country
Amah Gnassigbe	T.R.I.A.M.I. A nti-trichomonas anti-amibiases	Mar. 31, 1989	Lome, Togo
Carlisle R. Dolland	Adaptive reference voltage generator for firing angle	Jul. 19, 1983	Trinidad and Tobago
Sultanali M. M. Karim	Use of prostaglandins E and F for induction of labor	Nov. 04, 1975	Kampala, Uganda
George O. Okikiolu	Periodic structures in series of electronic components	Dec. 19, 1973	London, United Kingdom
George Murray	Corn-stalk harvester	Feb. 01, 1870	Alexandria, Virginia
Lloyd P. Ray	Dust pan	Aug. 03, 1897	Seattle, Washington
Wade Washington	Corn husking machine	Aug. 14, 1883	Huntington, West Virginia
Henry Brown	Receptacle for storing and preserving papers	Sep. 07, 1886	Madison, Wisconsin
Mulongo M. Mukena et al.	Air operated well pump	Feb. 02, 1988	Lurunbashi Shaba, Zaire
Patrick Chilufya Chimfwembe et al.	Optical multiplexer, demultiplexer and methods	Oct. 23, 2002	Zambia
Boaz Amon Mafarachisi, et al.	Liquid mahewu production	Jul. 14, 1982	Salisbury, Zimbabwe

Table 6: List of Early Black inventors by city, state or country

[40]

Potential Wealth and Resources Available to Black People

Africa is an enormous continent. Its total square miles of 11,608,000 miles could accommodate China, Europe and the United States (combined 11,260,616 square miles); with room to spare ^(African Studies Center)Africa is a home to almost a billion people. Africa leads the world in the production and export of cash crops such as groundnuts (peanuts), palm oil and kernels, cocoa beans, cassava, cashews, vanilla beans, sorghum, cloves and yams. Additional major crops are coffee, cotton, bananas, rice, rubber, sugar, and sisal. African countries are powerhouses in the export of livestock, producing two-thirds of the world's supply of camels. They rank third in the production of goats and are almost seventh in production of cattle and sheep.
1

West Africa produces over seventy percent of the world's supply of cocoa, therefore most companies that use cocoa depend on the soil and labor of Africans. Africa's reserve of the world's most important mineral wealth is enormous.

"Africa has 90% of the world's cobalt, 80% of the world's reserves of chrome, more than 50% of the reserves of gold, nearly half of the planet's reserves of platinum," and nearly all of the world's reserves of industrial diamonds outside the former communist sphere of influence. Africa has a lot more than the above strategic industrial minerals. The importance of gold in the international monetary system cannot be over emphasized. If African countries were to withhold their supply of gold, the world's exchange system would grind to a halt.

Africa's fuel mineral is also enormous. It has a third of the world's reserves of uranium, leads the world in the production of copper, phosphates, and radium. The continent's share of natural gas is growing fast; iron ore and tin are also produced in commercial quantities. Four African countries, Nigeria, Libya, Algeria, and Gabon are members of the OPEC. South Africa is the world's largest producer of gem diamonds. In terms of other minerals, Africa has 80% of the world's tantalum, its share of "precious stones are diverse, ranging from sapphires to topaz, from malachite to opal, from rubies to tanzanite."8 And others which cannot be listed here because of the scope of this project. The Western world is prime beneficiary of Africa's great mineral wealth.[2]

Mining provides about half the total value of Africa's exports and it is dominated by the West's multinational corporations. The reason for this is because mining is capital and skill intensive. And in the absence of adequate local technological and managerial skills mining in Africa continues to be the preserve of the Westerners. Today, if Africa's mineral and mining resources were to be denied the world, the industries of the Western world would virtually collapse. ^(Ezeh)

---

[1] Work Cited: Page 5 *www.gov.mb.ca/labout/immigrate.multiculturalism/2_1.html*
[2] Work Cited Page 6 http://*www.gov.mb.ca/labout/immigrate.multiculturalism/2_1.html*

Minerals	Patents granted	Percent of World Total
Andalusite	92	40% World reserves
Antimony	18,188	12% World's production
Arabic Gum	3,000+	Sudan 70% of World's production
Bauxite	2,545	11.3% World's production
Chromite	1,376	99% World's production
Cobalt	47,793	47.2% Worlds' production
Coltan (colombo-tantalite)*	48	80% World reserves
Copper	100,000+	13.5% World's production
Diamonds	2,075	52% World's production
Fluorspar	849	30% World's production
Gold	41,876	50% World's reserves 24.1% World's production
Lithium	51,553	Zimbabwe World's 2nd leading producer
Manganese	157	31.3% World's production
Natural Gas	11,487	7% of World's production
Nickel	100,000+	5% of World's production
Petroleum	42,785	12 % World's production
Palladium	22,156	48.6% World's production
Phosphate Rock	1,065	8% of World's production Morocco 2nd leading producer
Platinum	41,315	74% World's production
Ruby	992	Over 50% World's resource
Rutile	2,447	27% World's production
Tantalum	14,310	80% World's production
Tanzanite	8	Tanzania is the World's only producer
Titanium	100,000+	22.6% World's production
Uranium	9,641	20% World's production
Vanadium	59	50% South Africa of reserves, 30% World's production.
Vermiculite	2,413	50% of World's production
Zirconium	29,980	24% South Africa of World's reserves

Table 7: List of minerals, natural gas, petroleum & precious stones in Africa

Coltan, a mineral primarily mined in the Congo, is the essential ingredient in cell phones, laptops, computer chips, nuclear reactors and

[42]

play stations. Without it, the *telecommunications* industry would lose a major portion of its annual profits. What if Africa did not produce coltan or some of the other major minerals? How would that affect the world?

Africa is by no means, a poor continent; its mineral, and natural resources are worth trillions of dollars. Africa and its people and wealth will be the deciding factors in uplifting the continent as a whole. For instance, the minerals located in Africa have thousands of patented uses that would benefit Africa, its people and the world. See: **Table 7:** which shows Africa's mineral wealth as well as the number of inventions derived from the minerals (Amin, Africa in world mining geography). This table also shows some of the minerals mined in Africa. I have added the patents related to their uses, and the percentage of the world's known reserves that they constitute.

Black innovators, inventors, labor and the natural resources of African and Caribbean nations have helped to construct the foundation of the world's economy. The United States is currently the world's leader in technological development and that is due in part to the tremendous labor and creative genius of Black, White, Arab, Asian, and Native American people whose combined brain power and labor built the United States.

African, Caribbean & S. American Countries
Natural Resources

The Caribbean Islands, Central and South America have some of the most fertile land in the Western hemisphere. Below are some of the leading countries in agricultural growth: The United States, India, China and Russia are among the top countries with arable land (**NationMaster.com, Agriculture Statistics - Arable and permanent cropland (most recent) by country).**

Top 30 Countries in Arable land	Total in thousand hectares
1. United States	179,000
2. India	169,700
3. China	135,557
4. Russia	126,820
5. Brazil	65,200
6. Australia	50,600
7. Canada	45,700
8. Indonesia	33,546
9. Ukraine	33,496
10. Nigeria	30,850
11. Mexico	27,300
12. Argentina	27,200
13. Turkey	26,672
14. Pakistan	21,960
15. Kazakhstan	21,671
16. France	19,582
17. Spain	18,217
18. Thailand	18,000
19. Sudan	16,433
20. South Africa	15,712
21. Poland	14,330
22. Germany	12,020
23. Italy	10,825
24. Ethiopia	10,728
25. Burma	10,495
26. Philippines	10,050
27. Romania	9,865
28. Morocco	9,734
29. Bangladesh	8,484
30. Algeria	8,195

Table 8:   Top thirty-four countries with arable and permanent cropland
[44]

India, Brazil and Ecuador are among the leaders in the production of bananas (NationMaster.com, Agriculture Statistics - Banana production (most recent) by country). Currently over one thousand four hundred patents are related to the use of bananas.

Top 30 countries in banana production	Total Metric Tons
1. India	11,000,000
2. Brazil	6,339,350
3. Ecuador	5,000,000
4. Costa Rica	2,101,450
5. Mexico	1,802,280
6. Columbia	1,570,000
7. Burundi	1,514,000
8. Honduras	860,545
9. Cameroon	850,000
10. Panama	838,266
11. Papua New Guinea	680,000
12. Egypt	620,000
13. Bolivia	435,100
14. Dominican Republic	401,766
15. Martinique	321,454
16. Angola	290,000
17. Haiti	290,000
18. Madagascar	260,000
19. South Africa	250,000
20. Australia	230,000
21. Kenya	210,000
22. Argentina	175,000
23. Cuba	153,546
24. Guinea	150,000
25. Guadeloupe	150,000
26. Jamaica	130,000
27. Israel	129,000
28. Central African Republic	115,000
29. Morocco	110,000
30. Malawi	93,000
31. Nicaragua	91,636
32. Liberia	90,000
33. Saint Lucia	80,000
34. Zimbabwe	80,000

Table 9:   Top thirty-four countries growing bananas

[45]

In cotton production, India, China, and the United States lead the world. (**NationMaster.com, Agriculture Statistics - Cotton production (most recent) by country**). It is important to note that the United States established its dominance in cotton production through the unpaid labor of Africans. For centuries, India has relied on the inexpensive labor of millions of Dravidians. Over forty-seven thousand patents are associated with the use of cotton.

Top 34 Countries in Cotton production	Total Metric Tons
1. India	25,500
2. China	17,559
3. United States	12,500
4. Pakistan	8,350
5. Brazil	4,400
6. Turkey	4,200
7. Greece	1,700
8. Syria	1,300
9. Australia	1,300
10. Mali	1,050
11. Egypt	1,000
12. Benin	750
13. Turkmenistan	700
14. Zimbabwe	575
15. Cote d'Ivoire	500
16. Sudan	500
17. Argentina	475
18. Cameroon	475
19. Nigeria	450
20. Kazakhstan	450
21. Spain	400
22. Iran	380
23. Togo	350
24. Paraguay	350
25. Chad	325
26. Mexico	300
27. Burma	270
28. Zambia	240
29. Peru	184
30. Columbia	155
31. Mozambique	110
32. Uganda	90
33. Senegal	85
34. Afghanistan	85

Table 10: Top thirty-four countries producing cotton

The following chart shows the major cereal growing countries that not only produce food to feed their own people, but also use it to feed animals. Over one thousand-two hundred patents are associated with cereals (NationMaster.com, Agriculture Statistics - Cereal production (most recent) by country).

Top 34 Countries in Cereal production	Total in Metric Tons
1. United Arab Emirates	206
2. Guyana	185
3. Jordan	166
4. Kuwait	163
5. Benin	159
6. Belize	157
7. Sudan	156
8. Ghana	152
9. China	149
10. Syria	147
11. Ecuador	145
12. Vietnam	143
13. Iran	141
14. Lebanon	140
15. Chad	140
16. Burma	139
17. Egypt	138
18. Togo	138
19. Nigeria	137
20. Guinea	135
21. Peru	135
22. Bolivia	133
23. Cambodia	131
24. Mozambique	131
25. Libya	129
26. Burkina Faso	129
27. Pakistan	129
28. Chile	128
29. Central African Republic	128
30. Angola	127
31. Algeria	127
32. Niger	127
33. Cote d'Ivoire	125
34. Albania	125

Table 11: Top thirty four countries producing cereals

Peanuts are now grown for the hundreds of products that can be derived from them, thanks to the pioneering and scientific work of Dr. George Washington Carver. Below is a list of major countries **(NationMaster.com, Agriculture Statistics - Peanut production (most recent) by country)** that grow peanuts. Over four thousand patents are associated with the use of peanuts.

Top 19 Countries in peanut production	Total in Metric Tons
1. China	13,420,000
2. India	7,700,000
3. United States	1,880,000
4. Nigeria	1,510,000
5. Indonesia	1,130,000
6. Burma	710,000
7. Chad	450,000
8. Senegal	450,000
9. Ghana	440,000
10. Argentina	420,000
11. Vietnam	400,000
12. Sudan	370,000
13. Congo, Democratic Republic of the	360,000
14. Burkina Faso	320,000
15. Guinea	250,000
16. Brazil	220,000
17. Egypt	190,000
18. Mali	160,000
19. Mexico	90,000

Table 12: Top nineteen countries producing peanuts

Sorghum is a hardy crop, used for producing sugar and other by products. There are now over one thousand patents associated with sorghum which was first cultivated in Africa. (NationMaster.com, Agriculture Statistics - Sorghum production (most recent) by country).

Top 20 Countries in Sorghum production	Total in Metric Tons
1. United States	10,450,000
2. Nigeria	9,000,000
3. India	7,300,000
4.. Mexico	7,300,000
5. Sudan	5,190,000
6. China	2,870,000
7. Argentina	2,200,000
8. Australia	2,110,000
9. Ethiopia	1,700,000
10. Egypt	900,000
11. Niger	720,000
12. Tanzania	580,000
13. South Africa	380,000
14. Venezuela	330,000
15. Yemen	260,000
16. France	230,000
17. Columbia	170,000
18. Thailand	140,000
19. Italy	120,000
20. Spain	20,000

Table 13: Top twenty countries growing sorghum

Thousands of products are derived from soybeans. There are now over nineteen thousand patents associated with soybeans, thanks in part to the proficient scientific work of Dr. Percy L. Julian. (**NationMaster.com, Agriculture Statistics - Soybean production, (most recent) by country**).

Top 21 Countries in Soybean production	Total in Metric Tons
1. United States	66,780,000
2. Brazil	50,500,000
3. Argentina	33,000,000
4. China	15,390,000
5. India	6,800,000
6. Paraguay	3,910,000
7. Canada	2,260,000
8. Bolivia	1,850,000
9. Indonesia	820,000
10. Russia	390,000
11. Italy	390,000
12. Uruguay	380,000
13. Korea, North	360,000
14. Serbia and Montenegro	300,000
15. Ukraine	230,000
16. Vietnam	230,000
17. Japan	230,000
18. South Africa	220,000
19. Thailand	220,000
20 Uganda	170,000
21. France	130,000

Table 14: Top twenty-one countries growing soybeans

Sugarcane production relied heavily on the labor of Black people, particularly in Brazil, the Caribbean and the United States. There are over eight hundred patents associated with sugarcane. However, it was world renowned Black engineer and inventor, Norbert Rillieux, whose three patents transformed the sugarcane industry helping to generate billions of dollars from it's by products. (Faostat.fao.org).

Leading Producers of Sugarcane	Total in Metric Tons
1. Brazil	422,926
2. India	232,300
3. People Republic of China	87,768
4. Pakistan	47,244
5. Mexico	45,195
6. Thailand	43,665
7. Columbia	39,849
8. Australia	37,822
9. Indonesia	29,505
10. United States	25,307

Table 15: Top ten countries growing sugarcane

In conclusion, Africa, the Caribbean, Central and South America and many South Pacific countries, with their vast natural resources, can use the marketable eco-friendly innovations and inventions that have been uncovered through research to enhance their economies. Thousands of patents for peanuts, sorghum bananas and sugar cane have already been filed. The countries that produce these crops should make full use of these patents.

Pillars of American, Caribbean and South American Economies

The pillars of American, Caribbean, and South American economies from the seventeenth through the twentieth centuries include the following crops; rice, coffee, cotton, peanuts, tobacco, sugar and indigo crops. The success of colonial economies was built on the muscle power of enslaved Africans, Native Americans and White indentured servants. These crops, along with corn, wheat and alfalfa, laid the foundation for the rapid technological advancement of the United States in the nineteenth and twentieth centuries. The labor of enslaved Africans was also used to transform these colonies and their crops into world class markets. The African was therefore not just an enslaved worker, but rather an important and integral part of transforming the Americas, the Caribbean and Europe into wealthy and vigorous economic markets.

There is a relationship between patent ideas of Black men and women and the chief industries discussed above. More importantly, the labor that went into planting and cultivating rice, cotton, sugar, indigo and tobacco has an African connection. The labor of enslaved Africans made these crops the cash cow of the Americas and was largely responsible for the economic success of the colonies.

Black Inventors Role in Economic Growth

Name of Inventor	Patent or Invention	Date	Residence
Jo Anderson	(Unacknowledged co-inventor) of the McCormick's reaping machine	1834	Rockbridge, VA.
Lewis H. Latimer	Found the filament that extended the life of the light bulb.	1882	Boston, MA., New York, NY
Jan E. Matzeliger	Developed and earned patents for shoe making devices that revolutionized the shoe production industry. These devices catapulted the United States to the leader in the production of shoes.	1884-1907	Paramaribo, Suriname, Philadelphia, PA., Lynn, MA.
Elijah McCoy	Patented lubricating devices for machinery, trains, and ships. Enabled the U.S and western countries to run their machines and factories twenty-four hours a day, seven days a week.	1872-1915	Colchester, Ontario, Canada, Detroit, MI., and Ypsilanti, MI.
Norbert Rillieux	Granted patents for sugar refining process, evaporation and vacuum pans, 1841.	1841-1943	New Orleans, Louisiana,
Granville T. and Lyates Woods	Received patents for electrical dynamos and devices, including the "third rail" for trains.	1884-1907	Cincinnati, OH., New York, NY.

Table 16: Early Black inventors' role in economic

[52]

Today, people of African descent are quite visible in mainstream society. Their images appear on billboards, television screens, in print media, and of course on the internet. Ironically, some of the products that Black people advertise and consume have their roots in innovations and inventions by people who look just like them. Many Black people may not realize that the ideas, products, and services created by Black inventors are now generating billions of dollars, cedis, dinars, euros, francs, kwanza, naira, rand, real, pesos, pounds, won, yen, yuan, renminbi and rubles each year. For example, the Evaporating Pan, and the Multiple Effect Vacuum Pan Evaporator have both generated billions of dollars for the food, chemical, and beverage industries each year since Norbert Rillieux received his patents, over two hundred years ago, in 1843 and 1846, respectively. These machines are used to produce refined sugar from sugar cane and beets, make evaporated milk, and produce chemicals. What would a soda taste like without refined sugar? Thanks to Norbert Rillieux, the beverage industry doesn't have to ponder this question, as it continues to rake in astronomical profits.

Black people in the United States, Canada, the Caribbean, the United Kingdom and Europe are the descendants of ancient people who were located throughout Africa and parts of the Middle East. Many of the faces on the stone statues and paintings from Kamit, also known as ancient Egypt, are black. Numerous scientific, mathematical and spiritual innovations originated in Kamit, and quite a few, form the foundations of today's inventions. Just as important is the fact that Black people, kidnapped and forcibly removed from Africa, came from cultures that had a deep comprehension of the importance of nature, the use of plants and minerals, and scientific principles which led to the development of innovations and inventions both inside and outside Africa. These areas include agriculture, animal husbandry, blacksmithing, architecture, chemistry, education (transforming boys and girls into responsible men and women), furniture making and traditional medicine. Ancient African civilization also created governments over which kings, queen mothers and chiefs presided.

It is important to correct the myth that savages and uncultivated people were transferred from their homelands to save them and put an end to their suffering. The Africans brought to shores of the Americas retained their innate intelligence. The proof of this is the hundreds of thousands of inventions, patents, and trademarks that have been filed throughout the world by Black people.

Influence of Black Labor and Inventions on the World

Figure 2 Map of the World

One of the first books that impacted Black inventor research significantly was Burt McKinleys' *Black Inventors of America*. Below is an excerpt about Andrew J Beard, a Black man whose invention of the Automatic Car Coupling device had a major impact on the safety of railroad workers in the United States:

> The tremendous influence of the Black inventor upon American industry and culture is a force which is still structuring our society. In a May, 1969 decision, the United States Supreme Court once again underscored the viability of the contribution. This case, cited below, has such obvious relevance (and lends such vigorous support to positive evaluations of Black genius) that I am reminded of that familiar quotation: "Thou shalt not bear false witness against thy neighbor." It is an accepted fact that we are influenced, guided, and motivated by our Communications. For so many scholars, historians, and our culture-in-general to have deleted the magnificent accomplishments of an entire race... Is to collectives "...Bear False Witness."

[54]

Fortunately, many of these 'sins of omission" are being rectified at last. In 1962, the American Historical Association, along with two similar groups in England—The British Association for American Studies and The Historical Association of England and Wales—began an International Research Project entitled, "National Bias in School Books of the United Kingdom and the United States.

The "**Automatic Railcar Coupler**" was the focal point of the Federal Safety Appliance Act, which Congress enacted at the turn of the century. Andrew J. Beard, a Black laborer in Alabama freight yard, invented and patented this device in 1897 (US #594,059). This act made it unlawful for a railroad to supply cars which did not couple automatically on impact. So important was this invention to the development of America's huge railroad complexes (which supported a burgeoning, industrial society) that in 1908, Congress took an additional step by passing the Federal Employers Liability Act. This legislation gave railroad employees the right to sue in Federal Court when injured as a result of equipment failure---should such failure be a violation of the original Safety Appliance Act.

The specific case, cited this year, arose from injuries sustained by a workman in Iowa while helping load and move freight cars. The victim of the accident sued the railroad company, claiming that his injury resulted from a defective Coupler and that this defect violated the Appliance Act. The case decided against the plaintiff as he "was the employee of the Grain Elevator Company, not of the Railroad.

This case revealed, however, in detail, the entire social, economic, and legal pyramid which has evolved from the compassion – inspired invention of a Southern Black laborer. It might be well to point out that subsequent and similar legislation involving the safety and welfare of workers in mines, factories, building trades, and other fields, drew its form and substance from this pioneering concept of invention and human concern. Throughout the Industrial Nations of the worlds, we find similar legislation based upon this American Model.

The element of motivation, in relationship to achievement, cannot be over emphasized ! The author is able to recall, from his own black youth, the drive and determination to fully participate in the American Scene; enlightened and inspired the knowledge that so much of America's Scene was 'His Scene'. It was not an alien world of which he wanted no part—or that was rejected because it seemed to have no blackness, no soul!—but rather he was led to perceive just how much of the world bears the stamp of an Ebony Psyche—the thousands of inventions and innovations of America's Black. For him there could no longer be borne "False Witness!" [3].

Many western historians have traditionally omitted the fact that other cultures were using their own ideas and inventions to benefit their societies long before their contact with and dominance by Europeans. Take the cotton gin for instance. Eli Whitney is often credited with its creation; however, Africans, Chinese, Indians, Arabs and Native Americans had developed their own cotton gins.

In her book, *Inventing the Cotton Gin, Machine and Myth in Antebellum America*, Lakwete states in her preface that:

This study reopens the discussion. It explores the history of the gin as an aspect of global history and a facet of Southern industrial development. It begins with cotton the commodity the gin was invented to process, then examines gin invention and innovation in Asia and Africa from the first to seventeenth century, when British colonizers introduced an Asian hand-cranked roller gin to the Americas. First, indentured British and later enslaved Africans built and used foot-powered models to process the cotton they grew for export on mainland North America and in the Caribbean.

---

[3] Burt McKinley, Jr. **Black Inventors of America, page 1-2.**

Starting in the middle of the eighteenth century, cotton production increased in response to expanding textile production in Great Britain. Colonial mechanics correspondingly built water, wind-, and animal-powered models, all of which were types of roller gins. In 1794 Eli Whitney patented not the first but a new type of cotton gin.[4]

Black Inventors inducted into National Inventors Hall of Fame

As of 2007, the United States National Inventors Hall of Fame has inducted the following African Americans:

Year Inducted	Name of Inventor-	No. of patents
1990	Dr. George Washington Carver	Three patents[5]
1990	Dr. Charles R. Drew	Three patents
1990	Dr. Percy Lavon Julian	One hundred-five
1997	Mark Edward Dean	One hundred
1999	James E. West	Forty patents
2001	Elijah McCoy	Forty-seven patents
2003	Dr. George R. Carruthers	One patent
2004	Lloyd Augustus Hall	Fifty-four patents
2005	Garrett Augustus Morgan	Three patents
2006	Andrew J. Beard	Eleven patents
2006	Lewis H. Latimer	Ten patents
2006	Jan E. Matzeliger	Six patents
2006	Granville T. Woods	Over forty patents
2007	Emmett W. Chappelle	Fifteen patents
2007	Frederick McKinley Jones	Over thirty patents
2007	Alexander Miles	Three patents

Table 17: Sixteen Black inventors inducted into National Inventors Hall of Fame

Despite this number of Black American inductees, no Black women have been inducted into the National Inventors Hall of Fame. Women are not alone in being unfairly overlooked. In 1991, pioneer inventor, Frederick McKinley Jones, inventor of Thermo King refrigerated units, was awarded the National Medal of Technology, and in 2007 was finally inducted into the National Inventor Hall of Fame. In 1992, Walter Lincoln Hawkins, pioneer inventor for AT&T Bell Laboratories' plastic coatings for communication cables, used by telephone companies around the world was also a recipient of this prestigious medal. Although his was finally inducted into the National Inventors Hall of Fame. inventions saved telephone companies billions of dollars, he was not inducted into the National Inventors Hall of Fame.

---

[4] Angela Lakwete, "**Inventing the Cotton Gin-Machine and Myth in Antebellum America**", page viii
[5] Dr. Carver developed hundreds of products from peanuts, sweet potatoes, clay and plants.

Black inventors - Pillars of Industry

Inventors help to sustain the economic weight of the world. The list below provides a small sample of the Black Atlases, who through their discoveries, inventions, innovations and ideas, have made this world a better place.

The United States has a population of over three hundred million people; approximately, 12.9% of its population is of African descent. This calculates to over thirty million people. The United States is among the world leaders in the development of patents and trademarks, aided in part by the ideas, innovations and inventions of Black inventors.

Jelani Aliyu, a Nigerian born car designer, created the electric car called Chevrolet Volt. As power conservation in automobile design begins to become more described, this car could gradually help to revolutionize the automobile industry, 2007.

Dr. George Washington Carver, Diamond Grove, Missouri, Father of Agronomy, National Inventor Hall of Fame inductee. His pioneering work in peanuts, pecans, soil and plants revolutionized the use of plants and crops and provided an alternative to using chemicals. In 1933, Dr. Carver's experiments, research and product development of peanuts were responsible for Congress enactment of Section 22 of the Agricultural Adjustment Act of 1933, legislation passed to protect peanuts grown and produced in the United States. His pioneering work, saved lives and farms, and generated billions of dollars in income. Dr. Carver managed to patent only three of his ideas. If he had sought patents for all of his discoveries and works, they would number over one thousand. Dr. Carver is the "Father of the Peanut Industry" and the "Wizard of Tuskegee", patents, 1925-1927.

Mark Edward Dean, Jefferson City, Kentucky, (over 200 domestic and international patents), National Inventors Hall of Fame inductee. Dean also worked on the development of bus control allowing the control of peripheral processing devices for disk drives, video gear, speakers and scanners. Dean led the team that developed the first gigahertz chip that is capable of doing a billion calculations per second. He has received countless awards and recognition including the IBM Invention Achievement Award and the IBM Outstanding Innovation Award, patents 1981-2007.

Dr. Charles R. Drew, Washington, DC, father of modern blood plasma preservation and National Inventors Hall of Fame inductee. Dr. Drew was a pioneer in the medical use of blood plasma research. His great scientific and innovative work has saved millions of lives. Dr. Drew achieved many honors during his lifetime including three patents. He was also posthumously honored as one of the first African-Americans inducted into the National Inventors Hall of Fame in April of 1990; since his induction, fourteen black inventors have been inducted into the National Inventors Hall of Fame, patents 1942-1945.

Ralph V. Gilles, Lake Orion, Michigan, has nine design patents that have transformed car design for Daimler-Chrysler. Gilles was cited as Car Designer of the Year for the Chrysler 300, patents 1997-2005.

Lloyd Augustus Hall, Elgin, Illinois, received over fifty-eight patents related to meat curing compositions, solid seasoning, antioxidant flakes, and sterilization procedures for medical supplies. Many of his patents were assigned to Griffith Laboratories, Inc., patents 1933-1961.

Lonnie G. Johnson, Tuskegee, Alabama, awarded over one hundred fifty foreign and domestic patents, of Super Soaker™ Fame. His pioneering inventions revolutionized the water gun from an occasional warm weather toy into what is known as the 'Super Soaker™'. Mr. Johnson started his own company, Johnson Research and Development Co. His research has expanded to develop a number of new ideas and inventions, patents 1977-2007.

Frederick McKinley Jones, Covington, Kentucky (Thermo King) received over thirty patents related to refrigerated units for trains, ships, jet transports and buses. Mr. Jones was the founder of Thermo King, one of two commercial refrigeration companies. These refrigerated units are responsible for transporting fruits, vegetables, frozen foods, medical supplies and flowers among other products. Thermo King Units for preserving food products feed billions of people every year, and generate billions of dollars in commercial markets, patents 1942-1961.

Dr. Percy Lavon Julian, Americus, Georgia, (over 100 patents), National Inventors Hall of Fame inductee. His pioneering work transformed the soybean from just a feed crop for animals into an agri-crop, from which medicine, paints, lecithin, and fire extinguishing foams were developed. Dr. Julian started his own company, Julian Laboratories, in Mexico City, Mexico. He made sterols and other medication derived from soybeans and the dioscorea barbasco amarillo root. He sought to make medicines inexpensive for those who could not afford them, thereby making them readily available to everyone regardless of socio economic status. Dr. Julian is cited as being one of the greatest chemist/scientists of the top one hundred scientists of all time, patents 1941-1972.

Kofi Afolabi A. Makinwa's (Ghana) pioneering inventions have been used in Personal Data Assistants (PDA's) and computers. He has over fifty domestic and foreign patents, many of them assigned to U.S. Phillips Corp., New York, patents 1994-2007.

Jan Ernst Matzeliger (Suriname, Dutch Guiana), (six patents) Lynn, Massachusetts, National Hall of Fame inductee. Matzeliger pioneered and designed a revolutionary concept that enabled mass production of hundreds of shoes per day by a single shoe maker. Though Matzeliger only received five patents, his inventions have been used to make billions of pairs of shoes and transformed the United States, South America, Europe and the Pacific Rim countries into world leaders in the production of shoes. They also helped to propel the United States to at one time become the leading shoe manufacturer in the world. Shoe manufacture and production is a multi-billion dollar a year industry. Matzeliger's patents have been cited ten times in the United States Patent Office since his death, patents 1883-1891.

Norbert Rillieux, New Orleans, Louisiana, (three patents), National Inventor Hall of Fame inductee. His inventions, the Evaporating Pan and Multiple Effect Vacuum Pan, revolutionized the sugar industry. Rillieux's

[59]

devices are responsible for converting sugar cane, beet, and corn to sugar crystals, as well as making condensed milk, gelatin, paper, glues and countless other products. Rillieux's work has generated billions of dollars. His pioneering work in the use of steam technology is still used today, and his inventions are cited ninety-eight times in the United States Patent Office, patents 1843-1857.

Tisafaye Shifferaw, (Ethiopia) invented the "Bowflex™" and "Selectech™" which have generated millions of dollars since their introduction into the world of exercise equipment. Shifferaw has developed a number of other innovative exercise devices, and has started his own company called Dosho which specializes in exercise equipment, patents 1986-2006.

Samuel Ayodele Sangokoya, (Nigeria), has over fifty patents all of which are in the chemical industry. Many of Sangokoya's patents are assigned to Albamarle Corporation located in Richmond, Virginia, patents 1992-2001.

Herman W. Smith, Kalamazoo, Michigan, received over seventy patents for medical formulas, including countless patents that were assigned to Upjohn, 1978-1997.

Granville T. Woods, Cincinnati, Ohio (fifty patents), National Inventors Hall of Fame inductee. Woods' work revolutionized electrical railway systems throughout the United States and the world. The 'third rail' is one of Woods' most innovative inventions. Due to his work Woods is often referred to as the "Black Edison", patents 1884-1907.

The inventors above represent over four hundred inventions which generated jobs for millions of people and produced income in the billions of dollars in the world economy.

Black Inventors at Historically Black Colleges and Universities

There are one hundred and fourteen Historically-Black Colleges and Universities (HBCU) in the United States today. Most of these colleges and universities are located in the southeastern United States. So far, sixty-eight HBCU attendees and graduates have produced over seven hundred patents.

Name	School, location	Number of Patents
Patricia Bath	Howard University, Washington, DC.	Over nine patents
Sandra J. Baylor	Southern University, Shreveport, LA.	Over ten patents
Ernest B. Izevbigie,	Jackson State, Jackson, MS.	Three patents
Lonnie G. Johnson	Tuskegee Institute, Tuskegee, AL.	Over one hundred patents
Howard S. Jones	Virginia Union, Richmond, VA.	Over twenty patents
Louis W. Roberts.	Fisk University, Nashville, TN.	Ten patents
Archie Young	Lincoln University, Lincoln, PA.	Over twenty patents

Table 18: Black inventors from Historically Black Colleges and Universities (HBCU's)

Black Inventors at Colleges and Universities in the United States

Black inventors have also graduated from other national colleges and universities that are not HBCU's.

Name	School, location	Number of Patents
Patrica S. Cowings	State University of New York, Stony Brook, NY.	One patent
David N Crosthwait	Purdue University, West Lafayette, IN.	Over thirty domestic and one hundred international patents
Cortland O. Dugger	Tufts University, Boston, MA.	Seven patents
Francis Gaskins	Hunter College, New York, NY.	Four patents
Meredith Gourdine	Cornell University, Ithaca, NY.	Thirty-nine patents
Dr. George F. Grant	Harvard University, Cambridge, MA.	One patent
Dr. Lloyd A. Hall	Northwestern University, Evanston, IL.	Fifty-eight patents
Marc Hannah	Illinois Institute of Technology, Chicago, IL.	twenty patents
Marshall G. Jones	University of Michigan, Ann Arbor, MI.	forty-four patents
Barbara A. Nichols	Massachusetts Institute of Technology, Cambridge, MA.	One patent

Table 19: Black inventors from colleges and universities in the United States

Black inventors in the United States come from geographically diverse areas; small towns, medium-sized and major cities. For instance, the city of Boley, Oklahoma was founded in 1903 and incorporated on May 11, 1905. Boley, a small town of a few thousand people spawned a number of Black inventors who were granted twenty-six patents between 1918 and 2005. If we were to apply that same inventive effort to all of the hamlets, towns and cities inhabited by the more than forty million Blacks in the United States, this scale of innovation, as measured by patents and trademarks, expands tremendously. Metropolitan areas have also been centers of creativity for thousands of Black inventors, as is evidenced by the large number of patents and trademarks therein.

Figure 3 Map of the United States

Cities in the United States with Black Inventors

My research has uncovered information that supports the idea that Black inventors are not concentrated just in the urban centers of the United States. I have found Black inventors in cities and towns where the percentages of African Americans are below fifty percent.

Out of a total population of over three hundred million people, close to forty million African Americans, currently live in the United States. We also have to take into account the migration of Black people from Africa, Australia, Canada, the Caribbean, Central and South America, Europe, the Middle East and the United Kingdom into the United States. This widens the scope of inventions by Black people in the United States. For instance, my research shows that Black people from Africa, Canada, the Caribbean, and Central America have filed for and were granted patents in the United States. The earliest and greatest numbers of patents, however, have so far been granted to African Americans in the United States. Below is a brief list and description of patents granted to Black inventors.

[63]

Alabama

Willie A. Shields, Birmingham, received six patents for a bag handler, combination tools, bag-mounting appliance, garment bagging machine, 1919-1950.

Paul B. Ruffin, Huntsville, received five patents for devices for controlling optical twist on a bobbin and related inventions, 1986-1998.

Joseph F. Parker, Mobile, granted a patent for automatic fare-register, 1914.

Asouzu Moore Ugochukwu, Montgomery, created automated capillary electrophoresis method and apparatus (patent assigned to Troy State University), 2000.

Joseph C. Bagley, Selma, designed a wall tie, 1951.

John R. Cooper, Tuskegee, received four patents, on chemical compositions, 1966-70.

Alaska

JoAnn Greer, Anchorage, developed a patent for double bladed windshield wiper with a central sponge portion, 2003.

Arizona

Phillip A. Carswell, Tempe received three patents related to cryptography for telecommunication equipment, (patents assigned to Motorola), 1994-2000.

Emmanuel O. Nwadiogbu, Scottsdale, received five patents related to computer equipment (patents assigned to Honeywell), 2004-2007.

Adolphus Samms, Yuma Station, received eight patents for rocket designs, 1958-67.

Arkansas

John B. Mathis, Forrest City, co-inventor, granted a patent for automatic stovepipe damper, 1902.

Jesse C. Clamp, Helena, received a patent for curtain for refrigerator car doors, 1929.

James Henry Smith, Little Rock, granted four patents for peach-cutter, peach stoner, machine for stoning fruit and weather board gage, 1887-1909.

Emmanuel Moore, Pine Bluff, received five patents related to earth moving equipment and a fish feeder, 1958-1970.

California

Mufutau G. Olatunji, Berkeley, co-inventor received patents for continuous process for electro polishing surgical needles, 1998-1999.

Henry T Sampson, China Lake, received three patents including process for case bonding cast composite propellant grains, 1964.

Richard B. Spikes, Fort Bragg, granted patent for trolley pole arreseter, 1920.

Robert M. Bragg, Fresno, received a patent for a safety flow valve, 1958.

Franklin W. Baker, Inglewood, awarded patent for an anti-theft steering-wheel restrictor, 1994.

Dr. Keith Black, Los Angeles, received over ten domestic and foreign patents for medical procedures that have saved endless lives worldwide, 1994-2002.

Marc R. Hannah, Menlo Park, received over twenty domestic and foreign patents related to computer generated graphics systems, which are used in Lucas films™ and by countless other movie production companies for producing special effects, 1988-1998.

John L Jones, Sr. and Jr., Los Angeles and Pasadena, father and son have received over fifty patents for tampon applicators, sanitary belts, diapers, battery cases, room occupancy power reprogrammer among other inventions, 1946-1988.

Cyprian Emeka Uzoh, Milipitas, co inventor granted over twenty patents, including an apparatus for plating and polishing a semiconductor work piece, 2001-2004.

William A. Hill, Mountainview, awarded patent for a high resolution, high-speed digital camera, 1991.

Joseph T. Gier, Oakland, received six patents including method of making electro-magnetic wave reflector, 1950-1964.

Dr. Adrian Hightower, Pasadena, co-inventor of four patents including, LaNi5is-based metal hydride electrode in Ni-MH rechargeable cells, 2003-2004.

Robert L. Thornton, East Palo Alto, received over forty patents related to laser printing (patents assigned to Xerox Corp), 1987-2001.

Paul L. Brown, Redwood City, received several patents including, electric top, gyroscopic top, spinable string less top, 1958-1984.

[65]

Dennis K. Napier, Sacramento, invented an earth splitter, 1992.

Claude Q. C. Hayes, San Diego, awarded seven patents including heat absorbing temperature control devices and method, 1984-2001.

Boyd G. Watkins, San Francisco, received four patents including a synchronized watch movement, 1968-1993.

Forrest L. Wade, San Jose, received nine patents including a data storage system, (assigned to International Business Machines, 1974-2002.

Baila Ndiaye, Santa Clara, received two patents including enforcing file authorization access, (patents assigned Hewlett Packard), 2003.

Kenneth C. Kelly, Sherman Oaks, granted fourteen domestic and international patents including array antenna with slot radiators offset by inclination to eliminate grating lobes, 1991-1995.

Kunle Olukotun, Stanford, awarded five patents including dram power management, (patents assigned to Sun Microsystems, Inc.), 2003.

Effiong Ibok, Sunnyvale, received over forty domestic and international patents including method for establishing ultra-thin gate insulator using annealed oxide and oxidized nitride, (patents assigned to Advanced Micro Devices), 1995-2007.

Colorado

Michel Bowman-Amuah, Colorado Springs, received ten patents, including a patent for a managing information in an integrated development architecture framework, (patents assigned to Accenture LLP), 2002-2003.

Dewey S. Sanderson, Denver, awarded nine patents including urinalysis machine, 1968-1986.

Donna M. Auguste, Lyons, granted four patents including a method and apparatus for recognizing handwriting of different users of pen-based computer systems, (patents assigned to Apple Computer, Inc.), 1995-200.

Connecticut

Kenney U. Acholonu, Bridgeport, received three patents related to chemical compositions, 1979.

Henry Grenon, New Haven, received three patents for a clothing-related device, a can holder and razor stropping device, 1896-1908.

Narku O. Nortey, Trumbull, eight domestic and foreign patents related to development of various machines 1982-1992.

Delaware

Lyndon O. Barton, Newark, received four patents related to dual timing apparatus. bridge bidding aid, and time device, 1980-1984.

Dotsevi Y. Sogah, Wilmington, received twenty-five domestic and foreign patents from polymers, including 'living polymers' (assigned to E. I. du Pont, de Nemours and Company), 1985-1997.

District of Columbia

James T. Adams, Washington, received a patent for improvement in permutation-locks, 1871.

Joseph C. Dacons, Washington, received a number of patents for explosive compounds, (patents assigned to U. Navy), 1967-1977.

Howard S. Jones, Washington, received over thirty patents related to various types of antennae for the U.S. military 1962-1981.

Charles A. Peterson, Jr., Washington, received thirteen patents for power-generating equipment, water purification straw, and heaters, 1965-1991.

William H. Ross, Washington, co-inventor granted thirteen patents including process for preparing concentrated fertilizer, 1916-1928.

Florida

John H. Allen, Winter Park, received nine patents for computerized equipment for the United States Navy, 1968-1985.

Dwight D. Brooks, Boynton, received eleven patents related to telecommunication equipment (assigned to Motorola), 1991-1994.

Sharie Haugabook, Jacksonville, received a patent for methods of reducing beta-amyloid polypeptides, 2004.

Ivan Yeager, Miami, received two patents for artificial arm and hand assembly and locking device for redistricting the viewing of video cassettes, 1987-1990.

Yaw S. Obeng, Orlando, received over twenty domestic and foreign patents related to telecommunications equipment (assigned to AT&T and Lucent Technologies). 1994-2003.

Nathan R. Quick, Lake Mary, received over twenty patents for computer and laser technology (assigned to USF Filtration and Separations Group, Inc.,), 1998-2006.

Jerry M. Certain, Tampa, received patents for portable shampooing-basin, railroad nut-wrench, and parcel-carrier for bicycles, 1897-1899.

[67]

Georgia

Johnny G. Allen, Albany, received seven patents related to garbage bag rings and holders, 1978-2000.

Elbert Stallworth, Americus, received three patents for an electric heater, alarm clock electric switch, and an electric chamber, 1928-1934.

Chidi Okonkwo, Atlanta, received ten patents for automotive car and truck body designs, instrument panel and cockpit of a concept vehicle body, 2002-2004.

Charles A. Withers, Augusta, granted two patents for ventilator for ships, and a ventilator, 1903-1904.

John Elcock, Columbus, awarded patents for kiln and brick-kiln, 1904-1920.

Thomas C. Cannon, Jr., Dunwoody, received fourteen patents for a target position detecting device system and method, interactive television system, various optical fiber connector components, object locator system and methods, optical fiber connector, connector for optical fiber cable, interactive television system, remote controlled vehicle system, solderless electrical connector, 1975-1997.

Roderic I Pettigrew, East Point, granted patent for flow-induced artifact elimination in magnetic resonance images, (patent assigned to Georgia Tech Research Corp.), 1995.

Andrew J. Spain, Gainesville, co-inventor received a patent for a cotton cultivator and chopper, 1896.

Kwame Simon Ofosu, Lilburn, received a number of domestic and foreign patents including soft and strong thermoplastic polymer fibers and nonwoven fabric made therefrom, (patents assigned to Kimberly-Clark Worldwide), 1996-2001.

Artie C. Jenkins, Lithonia, awarded a number of domestic and foreign patents including optical cable having non-metallic sheath system (patents assigned to Lucent Technologies, Inc.), 1991-1997.

Jide Adedeji, Macon, granted five patents including method for removing stickies from wastepaper using modified cationic kaolin, and a method for making a reconstituted tobacco sheet (patent assigned to Nord Kaolin Co. and British American Tobacco (Investments) Limited), 1993-2000.

Thomas Mensah, Noscross, awarded thirteen domestic and foreign patents including a method and apparatus for coating optical waveguide fiber, 1988-1995.

Elwood G Ivey, Jr., Savannah, granted four patents including system for inhibiting use of a hand-operated machine by an impaired individual through detection of toxins in the individual, 1998-2001.

Hawaii

Cyriaque Kouadio, Honolulu, developed a method for surface shading using stored texture map (patent assigned to Square Co. Limited), 2002.

Idaho

Kwesi E. Abraham, Boise, awarded five patents including Internet print device font distribution method and web site, (patents assigned to Hewlett-Packard Company), 1995-2003.

Illinois

Billie J. Becoat, Alton, granted five patents for revolutionary bicycle designs, 1990-1993.

George H. Miley, Champaign, received five patents for plasma jet source using an inertial electrostatic confinement discharge plasma, spherical inertial electrostatic confinement device as a tunable x-ray source, plasma pumped laser, direct nuclear pumped laser, method and apparatus for producing complex carbon molecules, apparatus for applying layers of metal onto a surface, (assigned to U.S. Department of Energy Research and Development, Board of Trustees University of Illinois, and Daimler-Chrysler Aerospace), 1975-2001.

Andrew J. Brookins, Chicago, received twelve patents in the area of automatic train-control signal, and control devices, 1916-1924.

John E. Hodge, Peoria, received thirteen patents related to chemical compositions and baking control, (some of the patents assigned to Department of Agriculture), 1953-1978.

Akwete Adjei, Wadsworth, received fifteen patents for aerosol drug formulations, (patents assigned to Abbott Laboratories), 1989-2002.

Indiana

Maurice L. Danzler, Carmel, created a system using magnetic signatures to detect a vehicle event, and a system using information on a communications bus to eliminate magnetic noise, 2001-2002.

[69]

Omowoleoia Akinyemi, Columbia, co-inventor patented apparatus and method for processing wire strand cable for use in pre-stressed concrete structures and a premixed charge compression ignition engine with optimal combustion control, 1998-2002.

Brenda A. Truedell, Indianapolis, received two patents for antibacterial inventions, 1984.

Samuel G. White Jr., Fort Wayne, received a patent for a article of footwear with improved distribution closure system, 1988.

Robert W. Smith, Marion, granted patent for the reinforced stud support in fiberglass parts, 1980.

James P. Norwood, Gary, created a bread wrapping, labeling and sealing machine, 1916.

Lanre S. Ogundipe, South Bend, co-inventor, received a patent for heat resistant engine mount, 2000.

Joseph Ross, West Albany, created a hay press, bailing press and drill-hole reamer, 1899-1927.

Kevin T. Kornegay, West Lafayette, awarded a patent for incandescent light energy conversion with reduced infrared emission, 1996.

Iowa

Walter G. Madison, Ames, received two patents for adjustable radiator bracket and a flying machine, 1912 and 1932.

Robert N. Hyde, Des Moines, granted a patent for composition for cleaning and preserving carpets, 1888.

David N. Crosthwait, Jr., Marshalltown, received thirty patents related to vacuum heating, steam heating, refrigeration system, vacuum pumps, and apparatus for setting thermostats (patents assigned to C.A. Dunham) 1920-1966.

Albert Mendenhall, Oskaloosa, received patents for mechanical can opener, can opening device, a holder for driving reins, and for thill coupling, 1899-1925.

Kansas

John Arthur "Jack" Johnson, Ft. Leavenworth, received two patents for theft-preventing device for vehicles, and a monkey wrench, 1922.

William Douglass, Phillipsburg, received five patents for band serving knife, self-binding harvester band twister, carrier chain, band spout or trumpet including an earlier invention for an improvement in battery guns (machine gun) 1864-1905.

Fred J. Douglas, Topeka, created a valve block, 1914.

Ervin G. Greene, Wichita, patented guard for downspouts, 1931.

Kentucky

Hailey L Baker, Lexington, created a heater device control, 1886.

John H. Dunnington, Louisville, created a bulletproof safe, 1923.

Charles R. Clarke, Louisville, created the Kwanzaa utility tree, 2001.

Louisiana

William Hill, Alexandria, created a cotton-compress, and a choking mechanism for compresses, 1906-1915.

Edward Jones, Baton Rouge, created combined plumb and level, 1905.

Leonard Smith, Bastrop, patented a grain-door table, 1927

George R. Fox, Bogalusa, patented a design for brush, 1898.

John Baptiste Gustave Donato, Opelousas, patented apparatus for lifting water, game trap, liquid supply system, 1895-1896.

Samuel W. Harrison, Shreveport, received patents for contrast media dispensing apparatus, sterility maintenance cover and instrument support, surgical drape, closed system calculating device, pressure transducer elevation gauge, sterility maintenance cover, surgical instrument tray, and drape support and overlay mattress, 1992-2003.

Maine

William A. Johnson, Bangor, created a paint vehicle, 1888.

Robert B. Lewis, Hallowell, patented a machine for cleaning and drying feathers, and a manner of attaching bristles to the stocks of brushes for whitewashing and such other purposes, 1840-1841.

Maryland

John R. Moses, Annapolis, received patents for lubricating oil filter-refiner for internal combustion engines, inflatable pillow, and flat emergency exit sign utilizing an electro-illuminescent lamp, 1981-2001.

Emmett W. Chappelle, Baltimore, received patents for lyophilized reaction mixtures, disposable rodent trap, method of detecting and counting bacteria in body fluids, protein sterilization method of firefly, method of detecting cancer, (patents assigned to National Aeronautics and Space Administration), 1969-1983.

Olaleye A. Aina, Columbia, awarded patent for field effect transistor-bipolar transistor, darlington pair and patents for wavelength detection and photo-receiver technology, 1987-2005.

Thilivali T. Ndou, Gaithersburg, co-inventor, received various patents for shaving aids such as razor cartridges and cooling agents, (assigned to The Gillette Company), 1997-2001.

Joseph C. White, Hyattsville, received patents for an apparatus for determining specific gravity of an acid solution, fuel cell, and continuous water analyzer, (assigned to U.S. Army and U.S. Navy), 1947-1965.

Alfred G. B. Prather, Lanham, received patents for fan-like tail section and collapsible propeller for man-powered glider aircraft and various others including a prefabricated fireplace, 1971-1974.

Emanuel L. Logan, Jr., Silver Spring, received a number of patents for timing apparatus used to delay opening of doors, including emergency exit and security door mechanisms, (some patents assigned to Reliable Security Systems, Inc.,) 1981-1987.

Samuel A. Clark Jr., Wheaton, received patents for protective metal cap shield for plastic fuze radomes and a high pressure butterfly valve (patents assigned to U.S. Army), 1973-1976.

Massachusetts

Joseph Lee, Auburndale and Boston, received several patents including machine for mixing and kneading dough or analogous materials, 1894-1902

Kenneth A. Loftman, Boston, granted three patents including drying agent and process of making the same (patents assigned to Godfrey L. Cabot, Inc.), 1956-1963.

Emmanuel Ampofo, Boston, awarded a patent for a motorized newspaper dispensing system, 1998.

Cremora and William McCarty, Boston, granted four patents including wick raiser for lamps and improvement in flat irons, 1879-1881.

Nicodemus Tedla, Boston, patented a modulation of lir function to treat rheumatoid arthritis, (assigned to Immunex Corp.), 2003.

Aloysius O. Anaebonam, Burlington, awarded nine patents including pleasant-tasting aqueous liquid composition of a bitter-tasting drug, (patents assigned to Ascent Pharmaceuticals, Inc.), 1995-2000.

Robert P. Moses, Cambridge, earned a patent for games for enhancing mathematical understanding, 1996.

[72]

Olufeunmi L. Johnson, Cambridge, received eleven patents including composition for sustained release of human growth hormone, (patents assigned to Alkermes Controlled Therapeutics, Inc.), 1997-2003.

Abera Fura, Cambridge, granted several patents including compounds and methods for the treatment of cardiovascular, inflammatory and immune disorders, (patents assigned to Cytomed, Inc.), 1998-2001.

Benjamin F. Jackson, Cambridge, awarded ten patents including gas furnace, 1898-1906.

Cardinal Warde, Cambridge, received ten patents including method and apparatus for creating multiple phase level optical elements (patents assigned to Optron Systems, Inc), 1984-2002.

Jan Ernst Matzeliger, Lynn, granted five patents including lasting machine, 1883-1891.

Cortland O. Dugger, Newton, received five patents including solid-state laser employing a chemical reaction between a germinate and an oxide dopant, 1971-2002.

Louis W. Roberts, Roxbury, awarded ten patents for high frequency transmission control tube, (patents assigned to Microwave Associates, Sylvania Electrics and Metcom, Inc,) 1954-1968.

Edward Lewis, Springfield, granted a patent for spring gun, 1887.

Meshach Ojunga-Andrew, Springfield, earned several patents including one for adhesive compositions, 1997-2002.

Arthur Peters, Sudbury, granted over twenty patents including an arithmetic logic apparatus for a data processing system (patents assigned to Honeywell, Inc, and Bull HN Information Systems), 1981-1992.

Michigan

Allen H. Turner, Ann Arbor, received nineteen patents for the electro coating apparatus system and a number of related inventions, (patents assigned to Ford Motor Company), 1968-1972.

William A. Phillips, Comstock, created various furnace and incinerator systems and apparatus related to heating systems (patents assigned to Granco Equipment), 1972-1978.

Edward Akpan, Dearborn, received patents for method for producing self-lubricating powder metal cylinder bore liners, and accelerated thermal fatigue testing engine combustion chambers (patents assigned to Ford Global Technologies, Inc. Dearborn, MI.), 1998-1999.

[73]

Elijah McCoy, Detroit, awarded patents a number of revolutionary lubricating devices that changed the machinery, railroad and shipping industries. His patents for self-lubricating devices allowed the United States to transition to the forefront of industrialized nations, 1872-1915.

Joseph N. Blair, Detroit, received four patents including one for a wall and corner with grouted interlocked blocks, 1938-1958.

Samuel Admassu Gebremarium, Detroit, granted five patents including a method of depositing a metal film onto MOS sensors, 2001-2002.

McKinley W. Thompson, Jr., Detroit, granted patents for an automobile body and a toboggan, 1970-1975.

Thomas Flowers, Flint, created method of installing conduit, apparatus for installing conduit boring tool, and an accessory for distributing fresh water from a faucet to bathers, 1983-1986.

Oludele O. Poopola, Grand Blanc and Novi, received patents for various thermal spray coating mechanisms and ultrasonic welding device (patents assigned to Ford Global Technologies, Inc., Dearborn, MI.), 1997-2002.

Orville Z. Frazier, Grand Rapids, received patents for an internal combustion engine, combined rotisserie and attachments and hot air engine, miniature-racing car, atmospheric pressure engine with lateral support for burners, internal combustion engine, locomotive valve mechanism, carburetor, and humidifier for internal combustion engines, 1925-1966.

Minnesota,

Roger E Mitchell, Bloomington, created the physical therapy personal capsule, and a personal sauna with lighted hood, 1997-1999.

Roberts A. Harold, Eden Prairie, received patents for an optical switch with reduced reflection including connectors and construction methods and optical fiber crimp (patents assigned to ADC Telecommunications, Inc), 1991-1993.

Akintunde I. Akinwande, Minneapolis, co-inventor received various patents for making diaphragm-based sensors and apparatus constructed therewith, a field emitter liquid crystal display and backfilling method for producing a diaphragm containing microstructure, among others (patents assigned to Honeywell, Inc.), 1992-1998.

Robert S. Booker III, Minneapolis, granted patents for a method and apparatus for treating cardiac arrhythmia using auxiliary pulse, single pass

[74]

defibrillation/pacing lead with passively attached electrode for pacing and sensing and single pass lead system, (patents assigned to UAB Research Foundation), 1999-2003.

Mississippi

Ben Elwood Dyer, Clarksdale, received two patents, for a fuel mixer for internal combustion engines, and a ball-bearing fuel mixer, 1927.

James L. Hodges, Hattiesburg, received a patent for a slotted rotary shaver, 2000.

Ernest B. Izevbigie, Jackson, received two patents, for phyto-chemotherapy for cancer patients, and method for cAMP production (patents assigned to Jackson State), 2002-2003.

Augustus G. Jacobs, Jonestown, received various patents including devices for killing insects, combination locks, puzzle-map game, toy battle ship, winding-indicator for watches, and a roach trap among others, 1890-1911.

Peter T. Montgomery, Mound Bayou, received a patent for a ditching plow, 1892.

Michael O. Ezekwe, Vicksburg, invented a food composition comprising waterleaf leaves and methods of using thereof, (patent assigned to Alcorn State,) 2006.

Missouri

Neil E.S. Thompson, Sr., Creve Coure, received forty-two patents relating to chemical compounds used in chemical treatment, demulsifiers, corrosion inhibitors, drilling fluids, waxes and water treating chemicals, (patents assigned to Petrolite Corporation), 1977-1992.

Daniel Johnson, Kansas City, received three patents for lawn mower attachment, grass receivers for lawn mowers, and a rotary dining table, 1889-1890.

Walter L. Majors, St. Louis, received nine patents, including one for a hair dryer, coin controlled taxicab controller, motor-controlling devices for taxicabs and the like, oil stove, anti-skid device, mimeograph attachment, machine for the treatment of the scalp and hair, carburetor auxiliary or substitute, heating apparatus, heater for water-cooling apparatus of motor-vehicles and the like, 1913-1930.

Montana

William D. Davis, Fort Assiniboine, granted a patent for riding saddle, 1896.

Jerald Spencer, Helena, co-inventor, received two patents for portable power supply, power supply for portable computers and other electronic devices, 1996-1998.

Nebraska

William S. Campbell, Columbus, patent granted for self-setting animal trap, 1881.

Ayodeji J. Ayorinde, Lincoln, received ten patents including pressure vessel with damage mitigating systems, method of fabricating a filament wound structure, 1992-2002.

Harry K. Hillon, Omaha, received a patent for sash-lock, 1909.

Nevada

Chuko H. Ejiofor, Las Vegas, granted five patents including specific and reversible carbon monoxide sensor (patents assigned to FCI-Fiber Chemicals, Inc., 1994-1995).

Matthew Omofuma, Reno, granted a patent for the recovery of nickel from bioleach solutions, 1997.

New Hampshire

John T Gilmore, Jr., Amherst, granted four patents including a comparative visual assessment system and method, 1971-1999.

James E Hubbard, Jr., Derry, earned a total of thirteen patents including a patient monitoring system employing an array of force sensors on a bed sheet or similar substrate, 1986-1998.

New Jersey

Sacramenta G. Tankins, Atlantic City, granted two patents for comb and method of and means for treating human hair, 1920-1932.

Neville Holder, Cherry Hill, received several patents "N-T-butyl-androst-3-5-diene-17 beta-carboxamide-3-carboxylic" "acid polymorph A", "N-T-butyl-androst-3-5-diene-17 beta-carboxamide-3-carboxylic"" acid polymorph" (patents assigned to SmithKline Beecham Corp.), 1997-1999.

Percy C. Smith, East Orange, received eight patents related to telecommunications systems, (patents assigned to Western Electric Co., and Bell Telephone Labs.), 1925-1936.

Victor B. Lawrence, Holmdel, received twenty patents for digital transmission systems, (AT&, Bell Telephone Labs, Inc., Lucent Technologies, Inc.), 1983-2003.

Morris L. Smith, Lawnside, awarded patents for chemically treated paper products: towels, tissue, hygiene products containing odor neutralizing agents, improvements in cellulosic fibrous webs, (patents assigned to Scott Paper), 1989-1996.

Vincent A. Gill, Montclair, granted six patents for an assortment of valve inventions (patents assigned to Weatherhead Company and General Pneumatic Corp.), 1960-1974.

Lanny S. Smoot, Morris Township, received over fifty foreign and domestic patents for video telecommunication equipment, (patents assigned to Bell Communication Research and Telcordia Technologies), 1990-2000.

John B. Massey, Newark, granted patents for a surgical apparatus, and a sun visor, 1958-1960.

Vernon C. Wilson, Newark, awarded several patents including true self heating composition, 1972-1999.

Arnold F. Stancell, New Brunswick, received four patents, separating fluids with selective membranes, method of surface activation of non-polar hydrocarbon resins and printing, polymerization of olefin in a gravitating bed, flocculated microbial inoculants for delivery of agriculturally beneficial microorganisms, terephithalic and purification process, bonding thermoplastic resin films by means of radiation from a laser source, (patents assigned to Mobile Oil Corp.), 1967-1971.

Jesse E. Russell, Piscataway, received over thirty domestic and foreign patents for telecommunication, including apparatus and method for generating voice signals at a wireless communications station (patents assigned to AT& T and Lucent Technologies), 1996-2003.

Robert Allen, Plainfield, received patents for coin counter and wrapper, vertical coin counter tube, 1960-1965.

New Mexico

Godwin Okoye, Albuquerque, earned a patent for an arithmetic teaching machine, 1999.

Richard B. Spikes, Albuquerque, granted a patent for billiard cue racks, 1910.

[77]

Betty W. Harris, Los Alamos, received a patent for Spot test for 1,3,5-triamino-2,4,6-trinitrobenzene, TATB, 1986

New York

Adeyinka Adedeji, Albany, received seven domestic and foreign patents including, process for preparing polyhenylene ether thermoplastic resin compositions and articles made there from, 2000-2001.

Thomas Elkin, Albany, received patents for improved dining and ironing-table and quilting-frame, 1870-1879.

Hansel McGee, Bronx, received four patents for method for forming thin film electrical circuit elements by preferential nucleations techniques, N, n-diethyl and n-methyl, n-butyl docosyl succinamate, method of preparation of carbon transfer inks, method for forming thin film electrical circuit elements by preferential nucleation techniques, (patents assigned to International Business Machine Corporation), 1964-1965.

Derrick B. Mckie, Brooklyn, granted a number of patents including, glass fiber-reinforced oxymethylene polymer molding compositions having mechanical properties enhanced by amino-formaldehyde resin coupling agents, (patents assigned to Celanese Corporation), 1986-2001.

Herbert G. Bennett, Brooklyn, received patents for three dimensional objects and methods of making same, linked polyhedra with corner connector, gas range burner system, 1892-1923.

Oscar E. Brown, Buffalo, granted patents for horseshoe, detachable calk frame, non-skid vehicle tire, water motor, adjustable chain hook, 1892-1923.

Dr. Henry C. N. Clarke, Buffalo, received a patent for laparoscopy instruments and method for suturing and to ligation, 1975.

Dr. Carlton M. Truesdale, Corning, received over twenty domestic patents for related fiber optic connectors, couplers, compensator, waveguide among other inventions, (patents assigned to Corning, Inc.), 1989-2003.

Michael E. Croslin, Forest Hills, received fifteen patents for devices used in the hospital and medical industry (patents assigned to International Science Lab., Grumman Data System, Corp., Cros-Dorf Association, Technicon, Corning Glass and Medtek Corp.), 1966-1983.

Marvin C. Stewart, Hempstead, awarded nine patents including arithmetic unit for digital computers, (patents assigned to Sperry Rand Corporation) 1968-1976.

Cyprian Emeka Uzoh, Hopewell Junction, co-inventor granted twenty patents including method of forming an integrated circuit spiral inductor with ferromagnetic liner (patents assigned to International Business Machine), 1997-2002.

Christiaan C. L. Reeberg, Jamaica, granted patents for paint brush accessory, grease gun stand, and hold steady strap, 1979-1981.

Frank J. Ferrell, New York, awarded twelve patents including valves, 1884-1906.

Dorothy E. Hayes, New York, awarded two patents, for translucent structural panels and time-variable illuminating device, 1975-1990.

Tayo Olowu, New York, co-inventor of three patents including a computer-aided software engineering facility, 1992-1994.

Dr. Louis T. Wright, New York, received a patent for a device for treatment of bone fractures, (patent assigned to Harlem Hospital Surgical Research Fund), 1951.

John Yaw Ofori, Niskayuana, co-inventor awarded over twenty patents including method and catalyst system for producing aromatic carbonates (patents assigned to General Electric), 2000-2005.

William J. Knox, Rochester, received over thirty patents related to photography processing, Eastman Kodak, 1967-2002.

Morgan H. Morris, Schenectady, awarded four patents including a system for controlling spouted bed inlet conditions, (patents assigned to General Electric Company) 1982-1993.

William Barry, Syracuse, received six patents for stacking device, mail-cancelling machine, postmarking and canceling machines, door-hanger, and a postal machine, 1890-1897.

Dagnachew Birru, Yorktown Heights, granted over thirty patents including: frequency-domain equalizer for terrestrial digital TV reception and ATSC digital television system, (patents assigned to Koninklijke Philips Electronics N.V.), 1999-2007.

North Carolina

James Bauer, Asheville, received fourteen patents related to electronics for automobiles, (patents were assigned to Eaton Corp., and to Westinghouse Electric Corp.), 1970-2002.

Nnochiri Nkem Nekwurbie, Cary, co-inventor, granted domestic and international patents including conjugation-stabilized therapeutic agent

[79]

compositions, delivery and diagnostic formulations comprising same, and method of making and using the same, (patents assigned to Nobex Corp., and Protein Delivery, Inc.), 1984-2004.

Ernest L. Walker, Chapel Hill, received four patents for computer components (patents assigned to International Business Machine), 1972-1980.

Sidney Davidson, Charlotte, received a patent for a pants presser, 1908-1914.

Alonzo E. Parker, Jr. Durham, received seven patents for exercise equipment, oscillating reclining chair and shackling systems for live poultry 1981-1990.

Charles F. Harris, Fayetteville, received three patents for coin changer and control device, 1941-1942.

Lester Best, Jr., Greensboro, received two patents related to syringes, 1994-1997.

Ajamu Akinwande Wesley, Raleigh, received over twenty patents related to software development, (assigned to International Business Machines), 1998-2004.

William D. Polite, Wilmington, granted a patent for anti-aircraft, 1917.

David E. Agwu, Winston-Salem, granted a patent for cleaning and storage device, 1994.

Ohio

Joseph H. Tazewell, Akron, received twenty-six domestic and international patents related to chemicals used to make tires, (patents assigned to The Firestone Tire and Rubber Company, Akron, Ohio), 1965-1990.

Gilbert Farmer, Cincinnati, received twelve patents for gas turbine engines, and other related devices, (patents assigned to General Electric), 1997-2003.

Kofi Ofosu-Asante, Cincinnati, received over forty patents for domestic and international liquid or gel dishwashing, and fabric detergents, (patents assigned to Proctor and Gamble), 1992-2003.

Samuel Moore, Cleveland, received patents for vehicle a headlight, hobby horse, tire valve, and fuel-valve lock for motor vehicles, 1928-1935.

Harrison Allen, Jr., Cleveland, received two patents for method and apparatus for igniting solid propellants, 1971-1981.

James A. Parsons, Jr., Dayton, received six patents for ignition system, corrosion resisting ferrous alloy, treating silicon alloy castings, silicon iron,

iron alloy, cementation process of treating metals (patents assigned to Durion, Inc.), 1931-1949.

Charles R. Patterson, Greenfield, received patents for vehicle dash, thill coupling and furniture caster, 1887-1905.

Frederick A. Mosby, Shaker Heights, awarded ten inventions related to incandescent lamps, 1961-1970.

Donald B. Hopings, Toledo, granted patent for inspection apparatus, 1981.

Don A. Taylor, Wadsworth, received twenty patents including a heating system, solar siding for building and method of manufacture retreading tires, 1956-1982.

Edward L. Harris, Wilberforce, granted a patent for apparatus for handling corrosive acid substances, 1956.

John B. Christian, Yellow Springs, granted over twenty patents, for grease compositions, (patents assigned to United States Air Force), 1964-1984.

Oklahoma

Maurice W. Lee, Jr. and Sr., Boley, received fourteen patents for pressure cooker, electrical resistant cooking, and electrical cookers, 1950-2005.

Isaac Jefferson, Langston, received three patents for a cotton harvester, plow attachment, and a jack 1903-1905.

Henry B. Crichlow, Norman, granted nineteen patents including method of disposing of nuclear waste in underground rock formations, 1998-2005.

James W. Dulaney, Oklahoma City, received four patents for related computer hard disc drives, (assigned to Seagate Technology LLC), 2002-2003.

Edward H. Warren, Rentiesville, received two patents for train pipe coupling, and combined car and air-brake coupling, 1906-1915.

Volono H. Blauntia, Tulsa, granted a patent for window, 1937.

Oregon

Henry T. Chriss, Beaverton, received five patents for chemical bonding for footwear, (patents assigned to Nike, Inc.), 1994-1998.

Faye A. Briggs, Portland, received three patents related to computers, (patents assigned to Intel Corporation, Santa Clara, CA.), 2003-2004.

Henry W. Smith II, Tualatin, received over thirty patents for sneaker and shoe designs, assigned to Nike, Inc., 1997-2006.

[81]

Pennsylvania

Bridgette M. Budhall, Bethlehem, granted a patent for immersion lithography fluids, 2007.

Joseph R. Winters, Chambersburg, received two patents for improvement in fire-escape ladders, 1878-1879.

Harry Jackson, Harrisburg, granted five patents including burglar-alarm window guard, 1932-1939.

Mortimer B. Burgess, Lincoln University, received a patent for folding umbrella, 1903.

James C. Jones, Philadelphia, received four patents including grass trimmer, 1909-1923.

Cato T. Laurencin, Philadelphia, granted seven patents including biodegradable polymers for drug delivery in bone, 1994-2003.

Howard L. Scott, Philadelphia, awarded seven patents including method of lubricating or softening skin, 1972-1976.

Ronald R. Ambrose, Pittsburgh, received twenty-five patents including compositions and methods for coating food cans, 1985-2004.

Levi Ike Ezekoye, Pittsburgh, granted thirteen patents including an apparatus for separating and venting gas entrained in a liquid flow stream, 1977-1990.

Abdoulaye Traore, State College, awarded four patents including methods and tissue culture media for inducing somatic embryogenesis, agrobacterium-medicated transformation and efficient regeneration of cacao plants, 1999-2001.

Rhode Island

Abraham Pugsley, Jamestown, granted four patents including blind-stop, 1890-1891.

David B. Allen, Newport, awarded two patents for adjustable beds, 1912-1914.

Donald L. Stanford, Pawtucket, received a patent for technique for secure network transactions, 2001.

Arthur E. Pryde, Providence, earned three patents for portable sound manifold, 1973.

Donald H. Samuels, Warwick, awarded six inventions including a toy dump truck and toy race track for miniature cars (patents assigned to Hasbro Industries, Inc.), 1980-1983.

[82]

South Carolina

Charlotte Barnwell, Beaufort, granted a patent for folding bath stand, 1885.

Aiken C. Taylor, Charleston, granted nine patents including, combines, cotton planter and fertilizer distributor, 1906-1918.

Roy J. Moore, Columbia, awarded several patents for split tool mechanical vibrator, split workhead, clamp arrangement for track lifting and aligning device, 1986-1996.

Alexander B. B. Harris, Georgetown, created an automatic cistern cut-off and self-cleaning filter, 1903.

Edinburgh Graham, Orangeburg received two patents for trouser press and trousers creaser and presser, 1904.

Asa Thompson, Spartanburg, awarded two inventions, automatic hoe and cotton chopper and cultivator, 1906-1914.

George W. Murray, Sumter, received fifteen patents including a potato digging machine, planter and cotton seed planter, 1894-1908.

Tennessee

Percy Jackson, Chattanooga, patented a technique for a closure plug for pipes, 1927.

Francis E. Levert, Knoxville, granted over fifteen patents, including manual automobile pusher, thermal neutron detector and system using the same, portable feet elevator, spring cushioned shoe, 1982-2003.

Robert L. Horsley, Memphis, created mophead, bale-tie buckle, press for making mops, mop, insect swatter, clothes pin, pocket-knife, 1901-1942.

Dr. Ernest P. Alleyene, Nashville, granted a patent for an obstetrical appliance, a device which will take the place of six other instruments in obstetrical surgery, 1926-1943.

Texas

Olubunmi Adetutu, Austin, received over twenty domestic and foreign patents related to the telecommunication, (patents assigned to Motorola, Inc.), 1999-2004.

Vincent M. McNeil, Dallas, granted patents for selective area halogen doping to achieve dual gate oxide thickness on a wafer, method to enhance the formation of nucleation sites on silicon structures and an improved silicon structure, integrated circuit transistors, (patents assigned to General Motors Corp., and Texas Instruments, Inc.), 1998-2002.

Olayinka E. Ogunro, DeSoto, granted seven patents including device to foster cosmetically pleasing healing of nail bed tissue and mechanized hair braiding apparatus, 1982-2000.

Charles E. Lewis, El Paso, awarded two patents including pressure actuated electrical tire signal and electrical switch, 1941-1942.

John H. Woodberry, Fort Bliss, earned two patents for a support and pressure indicator, 1933-1935.

Roy J Jackson, Houston, awarded fourteen patents including rapid curing epoxy resin adhesive composition, (patents assigned to Shell Oil Company), 1991-1999.

Theophilus Ealey Neal, Prairie View, received three patents including a shower bath spray, 1932-1940.

Henry F. Stillwell, San Antonio, granted two patents for delivery of mail and other matter from aeroplanes while in motion, and means for receiving mail and other matter on aeroplanes while in motion, 1932-1933.

Gerald Rogers, Sugarland, co-inventor awarded nine patents including multiple digital processor system (patents assigned to Texas Instruments), 1978-1985.

Utah

Funsho K. Ojebuoboh, Midvale, granted a patent for refining of bismuth, 1993

Nosa Agbonkonkon, Provo, earned a patent for a cross-flow ion mobility analyzer (patent assigned to Becton Dickinson Co.), 2005.

Emmanuel O. Akala, Salt Lake City, UT., received a patent for Ph sensitive hydrogels with adjustable swelling kinetics for colon specific delivery of peptides and proteins (patent assigned to University of Utah Research Foundation), 1998.

Vermont

Ebenezer Eshun, Essex Junction, received three patents for computer inventions, (patents assigned to International Business Machines), 2004-2005.

Virginia

Thomas Tucker, Alexandria, received various patents for surface hardening by particle injection into laser melted laser beam linear adjustable integrating mirror, method of bonding and electrically conductive material to an electrically conductive layer which overlies a curved non metallic substitute, (patents assigned to U.S. Navy), 1981-1986.

Emmanuel L. Logan, Jr., Arlington, received countless patents for emergency doors, exit latches, emergency sign, 1971-1984.

Ernst W. Smaw, Chesapeake, created ink bottles, 1917.

Stanley E. Woodard, Hampton, received patents for several innovative medical devices, (patents assigned to National Aeronautics and Space Administration), 2002-2005.

Charles E.B. Burney, Newport News, developed a ship for carrying liquid cargoes in bulk, 1907.

Charlesworth R. Martin, Norfolk, co-inventor, granted a patent for vehicle door guide, 1991.

George J. Richardson, Petersburg, received a patent for combined trash receptacle and advertising carrier, 1922.

Charles L. Kee, Portsmouth, awarded ten patents including aircraft planted mine and anchor, 1911-1952.

Paul E. Williams, Purcellville, earned patents for airborne vehicles, 1971.

Aiken C. Taylor, Richmond, earned a patent for a window, 1917.

Mary B. Kenner, Williamsburg, received a number of patents including a carrier attachment for invalid walkers, 1976.

Washington

Cyprian Okwara Ogbu, Bellevue, awarded six patents including a beta-sheet mimetics and use thereof as inhibitors of biologically active peptides or proteins, (patents assigned to Molecumetics, Ltd.), 1998-2004.

Kedrich Jackson, Comas, received four patents including wet wiping system for inkjet printers, (patents assigned Hewlett-Packard Company), 1998-2001.

Nosakhare D. Omoigui, Redmond, granted four patents including system and method for knowledge retrieval, management delivery and presentation (patents assigned to Microsoft Corp.), 2002-2003.

Betsy Ancker-Johnson, Seattle, awarded five patents including solid state data storage and switching devices, 1965-1976.

Frank E. Foy, Seattle, earned a patent for wheel of Black history game device, 1992.

West Virginia

Virgil E. Matthews, Charleston, awarded six patents including polyurethane hydrogel fibers and tapes and composites with natural and other synthetic fibers or films, (patents assigned to Union Carbide Corp.), 1961-1976.

Samuel Moore, Fairmont, received patents for two inventions self-directing headlight and a headlight, 1926-1927.

William Hale, Litwar and McDowell County, granted patents for a motor vehicle, aeroplane and an improvement in aeroplane, 1925-1928.

Richard W. Wallace, McClean, awarded four patents including lash lamp pumped dye laser, 1973-1990.

Wisconsin

Henry Brown, Madison, granted patent receptacle for storing and preserving papers, 1886.

David E. Ford, Jr. Milwaukee, received ten patents, including a patent for a current limit control for direct current motors, (patents assigned to Allen-Bradley Company), 1963-1973.

United States Cities and the Number of Black inventors Researched

The African-American population is concentrated in the large cities of the Southeast, Southwest, Northeast, Midwest and West Coast. The following cities have produced Black inventors. Keep in mind that these are inventors who have been tracked to date; research in this area continues.

City	State	Patents
Akron	Ohio	Twenty
Albany	New York	Twenty-five
Anchorage	Alaska	One
Ann Arbor	Michigan	Thirty-five
Atlanta	Georgia	Fifty-nine
Austin	Texas	One hundred fifty-nine
Baltimore	Maryland	Eighty-three
Baton Rouge	Louisiana	Sixty-three
Birmingham	Alabama	Ten
Boley	Oklahoma	Twenty-seven
Boston	Massachusetts	Sixty-four
Brooklyn	New York	Seventy-three
Charleston	West Virginia	Five
Chicago	Illinois	Three hundred eighty-three
Cincinnati	Ohio	Two hundred forty-five
Cleveland	Ohio	Forty one
Colorado Springs	Colorado	One hundred
Derry	New Hampshire	Eleven
Detroit	Michigan	One hundred twenty-five
Essex Junction	Vermont	Two
Hallowell	Maine	Two
Houston	Texas	One hundred twenty-five
Indianapolis	Indiana	Thirty-four
Kalamazoo	Michigan	One hundred sixteen
Knoxville	Tennessee	Twenty
Lantana	Florida	Forty
Lincoln	Nebraska	Thirteen
Los Angeles	California	One hundred sixteen
Louisville	Kentucky	Thirteen
Marshalltown	Iowa	Thirty-six
Memphis	Tennessee	One Hundred forty-one
Milwaukee	Wisconsin	Ninety-eight
Minneapolis	Minnesota	Forty-four
Montclair	New Jersey	One hundred twenty-seven
New Haven	Connecticut	Nine
New Orleans	Louisiana	Twenty-two

New York	New York	Two hundred sixty-one
North Charleston	South Carolina	Thirty-six
Pasadena	California	Ninety-four
Philadelphia	Pennsylvania	One hundred sixty-seven
Phillipsburg	Kansas	Five
Pine Bluff	Arkansas	Twenty-three
Richmond	Virginia	Twenty-six
Rochester	New York	One Hundred sixty-six
Rosedale	Mississippi	Nineteen
San Diego	California	Forty-six
San Francisco	California	Thirty-one
Seattle	Washington	Forty
St. Louis	Missouri	Seventy-five
Tempe	Arizona	Twenty-four
Washington	District of Columbia	Three hundred eighteen
Wilmington	Delaware	One hundred sixty-two

Table 20: Black inventors in cities throughout the United States

Native American Inventors

As a bonus I have introduced some preliminary research on Native American inventors. We can't forget that Central and South America, Canada, and the Caribbean, were at one time occupied strictly by Native Americans. There are literally untold numbers of inventions, innovations and ideas that we now employ because of Native American culture and ideas.

Inventor	Invention	Date of Patent	City/State
Sarah Seeney-Sullivan	Board game incorporating Native American symbols and knowledge	Jan. 03, 1995	Chesworld, Delaware
William W. Millam	Ironing board	Jun. 1922	Okfuskee County, Oklahoma
William W. Milam	Attachment for gin feeders	Mar. 12, 1918	Alex, Oklahoma
Robert D. Blackstone	Trolley harp	Sep. 20, 1910	Muscogee, Oklahoma
John Patterson	Intrenching tool	Apr. 29, 1984	Fort Supply, Oklahoma
Francis E. Burgevin	Wrench	Jun. 19, 1894	Burgevin, Oklahoma
William D. Williams	Ribbon holding and winding device	Nov. 06, 1900	Chelsa, Oklahoma
Samuel I. Fields	Car-coupling	Oct. 23, 1888	Cherokee Nation, Oklahoma
Robert R. Majors	Tone arm head	Jan. 16, 1951	Muskogee, Oklahoma

Table 21: Brief table of Native American inventors

Though the names above are not traditional Native American names, the research so far clearly indicates that patents were granted to Native Americans in the nineteenth century, the twentieth century and beyond. Further research on the impact of Native American technology on inventions in the Western Hemisphere needs to be done. For more information please read *Indian Givers, How the Indians of the Americas Transformed the World,* by Jack Weatherford.

Black Women Innovators and Inventors

Since the beginning of time, Black women have played a key part in the nurturing of ideas, and the use of inventions. In Ancient Egypt (Kamit), Black women, working with science through meditation and trance, and understanding the role of nature in the area of reproduction and cultivation, took simple grasses and developed the grains (wheat, barley, millet and corn) that have fed the world for thousands of years. Black women's keen insight into mundane and spiritual laws, continues to give them the ability to assume the roles of queen mothers, chiefs, priestesses, presidents, heads of state, prime ministers, mayors, senators, congresswomen, leaders, businesswomen, doctors, lawyers, healers, scientists and inventors in their societies. All great civilization can be measured by their treatment of women and the education of the children.

The number of innovations, inventions, and trademarks by Black women has not been fully explored. We cannot just count the number of patents or trademarks, but must also consider that the ideas of Black women have helped to change the world and continue to today. For this information, we must explore the past. My research has uncovered over four hundred patents awarded to Black women. This list is still in its early stages. Some of the first Black women to file for patents were Martha Jones, of Ameilia County, Virginia, who received a patent for an improvement in the corn-husker, sheller on May 05, 1868. Mary Jones De Leon of Baltimore, Maryland who was awarded a patent for an improvement in cooking apparatus on May 16, 1873. Judy W. Reed of Washington, DC who was granted a patent for a dough kneader and roller on Sept. 23, 1884 and Sarah Goode of Chicago, Illinois, who received a patent for a folding cabinet chair on July 14, 1885.

Black women innovators and inventors worked side by side with their male counterparts. There is a clear indication of cooperation among civic leaders, businessmen, businesswomen and inventors. For instance, Annie E. Turnbo, of St. Louis, Missouri, the millionaire hair and beauty product entrepreneur had two inventions by Walter L. Majors of St. Louis,

Missouri, assigned to her name. The patents were for a coin-controlled taxicab-controller on August 05, 1913 and a hair dryer on Jan. 05, 1915.

Prolific Black Women Innovators and Inventors

Sylvia Adae-Amoakoh, Binghamton, New York, co-inventor patented three photographic developing compositions and use thereof in the processing of photographic elements, capacitor laminate for use in a printed circuit board and as an interconnector, method of making a parallel capacitor laminate, 1996-2003.

Betsy Ancker-Johnson, Seattle, Washington, earned six patents for signal generators using semiconductor material in magnetic and electric fields, radiant energy optical detector amplifier signal generator, detector-modulator for an optical communication system, solid state data storage and switching devices, and fast sequential switch with adjustable delay, (patents assigned to The Boeing Company), 1965-1975.

Patricia E. Bath, Los Angeles, California, earned a B.A. from Hunter College, New York and a Medical Degree from Howard University, Washington, D.C., developed the Laserphaco probe that could destroy cataracts. She went on to develop eight other devices, including one using ultrasound. Dr. Bath has nine patents from 1988-2003, and has been nominated to the National Inventors Hall of Fame.

Sandra J. Baylor, Ossining, New York, a graduate of Southern University, Shreveport, LA., employed at International Business Machine (IBM). Taylor's work in computers has earned her co-inventor status for ten patents from 1994-2001.

Bertha Berman, New York, New York, received five patents for tooth brush protector, bed sheet construction, fitted bed sheet construction and table cover, 1939-1971.

Joan Iyabo Amienmenaghene Campbell, Cambridgeshire, United Kingdom, awarded nine international patents related to fowl and avipox virus promoters, 1989-1993.

Francis E. Amoah, Cardiff, United Kingdom, co-inventor of ten domestic and international patents related to tissue treatment systems, electrosurgical method and electrosurgical generators, 2000-2004.

Relva C. Buchanan, Champaign, Illinois, co-inventor of four patents, low temperature of PZT, zirconia, and alumina ceramics, 1971-2001.

Dannette Connor-Ward, Olivette, Missouri, co-inventor of six patents including a method for soybean transformation and regeneration, sugar beet regeneration and transformation, efficiency soybean transformation protocol, (patents assigned to Monsanto Company), 1995-2001.

Christine Vonicle Mann Darden, Monroe, North Carolina, a graduate of Hampton Institute, a physics major and mathematics minor, Masters in mathematics from Virginia State. Darden later earned her PhD in mechanical engineering from George Washington University. She was employed at National Aeronautics Space Administration, Langley Research Center, Hampton, Virginia. Darden's outstanding work in wing design, supersonic flow, flap design, and sonic boom prediction led to over fifty technical papers. In addition, her work is cited in United States patents: 6464171, 6588703, 6942178, 2002-2005.

Bettye W. Greene, Fort Worth, Texas, a graduate of Tuskegee University, Greene developed a number of chemical processes related to latex paints (patents assigned to The Dow Company), 1984-1987.

Majorie Stewart Joyner, Chicago, Illinois, received two patents for a scalp protector and the permanent-waving machine, (patents assigned to the Madame CJ Walker Manufacturing Co), 1928-1929.

Elizabeth Wolde-Mussie, Laguana Nigel, California, co-inventor, awarded sixteen patents for medical pharmaceutical products and methods for reducing intraocular pressure in the mammalian eye by administration of chloride channel blockers (patents assigned to Allergen, Inc.), 1996-2002.

Christine Nare, Ouagadougou, Burkina Faso, received a patent for a formula to derive alcoholic drinks from cereals and fruit, 2001.

Florine Newell, Chicago, Illinois, co-inventor of seven patents for hair relaxer cream, conditioning hair relaxer system, (patents assigned to Johnson Products Co.), 1990-1995.

Dr. Amina Odidi, Ontario, Canada, earned her Bachelor of Science in Pharmacy from Ahmadu Bello University, Nigeria, and her PhD from the University in London, in the United Kingdom. She is the founder, President, COO and Co-Chief Scientific Officer of IntellPharmaceutics Corp., Mississauga, Ontario, Canada. She is an inventor and co-inventor who has received ten patents related to controlled-release drug products, (patents assigned to IntellPharmaceutics Corp), 2001-2004.

Gwendolyn Rolle, Freeport, Bahamas, was named Inventor of the Year, 2003 for her shoe accessory, shoe with interchangeable covers, 2007.

Saiyya Shabazz-Houston, Philadelphia, Pennsylvania, granted three patents including sanitary napkin with adjustable length intergluteal strip, 2002-2004.

Madame CJ Walker, Delta, Louisiana, developed a number of hair care products as well as factories for producing her products. Walker developed a system for selling her products and became a millionaire. Walker traveled to the Caribbean and Central America promoting her products. Mme. C.J. Walker has several hair dressing trademarks for hair salves and toilet preparations, 1906-1919.

List of Black Women Inventors by City/State or Country

Inventor	Invention	Date of Patent	City/State/Country
Valerie Adegbite, et al.	Electromagnetic curing apparatus and method of use	Apr. 11, 1995	East Lansing, Michigan
Maria Dolapo Adewunmi, et al.	Process for eliminating labile clycohaemoglobin from sample	Apr. 14, 1994	London, United Kingdom
Desire Afidegnon	Maracuja passion fruit syrup	Jan. 01, 2001	Lome, Togo
Francine Agbossou, et al.	Method for preparing optically active alpha-substituted benzyl alcohols	Sep. 12, 2000	Libercourt, France
Tanya R. Allen	Undergarment with a pocket for releasably securing an absorbent pad	Jul. 05, 1994	Detroit, Michigan
Jennifer Atkins	Hair maintenance cap	Dec.26, 1995	Oakland, California
Rosalyn Baxter-Jones	Devices and methods for cervix measurements	Apr. 17, 2002	San Diego, California
Annette B. Bell	In-dash compact disc retriever	Mar.17, 2001	St. Louis, Missouri
Jean-Marie Gueye, et al.	Method of identifying the owner of a smart card, uses internal memory to store biometric data which is displayed on request on screen into the card	Dec. 06, 2002	La Ciotar, France
Angela M. Hodge-Miller	Analog to digital converter using sawtooth voltage signals with differential comparator	Aug. 03, 2006	White Plains, Maryland
Christine Mayambala-Mwanika	Ascorbate interference-resistant composition, device and method for the determination of peroxidatively active substances	May 6, 1986	Mishawaka, Indiana
Geraldine Mbamalu	Oligomerized receptors which affect pathways regulated by trans-memberane ligands for elk-related recptor tyrosine	Nov. 15, 1998	Toronto, Canada
Robin Ndagijimana, et al.	Screen, especially for the seat of a motor vehicle	Apr. 08, 2004	Neuss, Germany
Vangile Ndlovu, et al.	A method of protecting plants against viral infections	Mar. 25, 1992	Cape Town, South Africa
Juliet Lorde, et al.	Determining and tracking downhole particulate deposition	Jan. 25, 2007	Port of Spain, Trinidad and Tobago

Table 22: Black Women inventors by city, state or country

[94]

Although Oprah Winfrey does not personally have any patents, seven inventions include her name in their descriptions. See United States Patents: 5633683, 6481012, 6428004, 6915528, 6219042, 5832472, and 5822123.

Oprah Winfrey™, Chicago, Illinois has sixty-one trademarks including her own television show. Oprah has starred in or produced: *Bee Movie, Charlotte's Web, Our Friend, Martin, Beloved, There Are No Children Here, The Women of Brewster Place, Native Son, The Color Purple*. Including her own talk show, any product that Oprah has advertised, promoted or endorsed has earned millions of dollars. Oprah, whose mission involves using truth, facts and compassion to educate and uplift her audience, has taken the high road to success. She seeks to improve the lives of people through her generosity − from aiding victims of Hurricane Katrina in Louisiana and Mississippi, to opening schools and providing resources to deserving people nationally and internationally. Oprah has also raised over fifty million dollars through her Angel Network for charitable programs.

Cathy L. Hughes of Washington, DC, has successfully owned and operated radio and television networks. Ms. Hughes currently owns sixteen trademarks on her TV-One Television Production company and has held over forty trademarks with her Radio One, Inc. She revolutionized the Black television industry recently with the re-broadcast of *Roots*. Using on-air commercials, she encouraged African Americans to rediscover their countries of origin through DNA testing. She has breathed new life into broadcasting for Black people in the United States, offering high quality programming such as documentaries, interviews, movies, and sitcoms through her network.

The following cities have produced the most Black women inventors. Keep in mind that these are the inventors who have been tracked to date; research in this area continues.

World cities and the number of Black women inventors researched

City	State or Country	Patents
Abidjan	Cote D'Ivoire	Six
Antananarivo	Madagascar	Two
Augusta	Georgia	Six
Austin	Texas	Four
Bamako	Mali	One
Benin City	Nigeria	One
Bessemer	Alabama	Two
Bohicon	Benin	Three
Cambridge	Massachusetts	Thirteen
Cambridgeshire	United Kingdom	Nine
Charlesville	Liberia	One
Chicago	Illinois	Sixteen
Christ Church	Barbados	One
Conkary	Guinea	One
Dakar	Senegal	Six
Detroit	Michigan	Seven
Franklin	Kentucky	Two
Hampton	Virginia	Ten
Harare	Zimbabwe	One
Holly Springs	Mississippi	One
Indianapolis	Indiana	Nine
Jacksonville	North Carolina	Two
Kingston	Jamaica	Six
Kinshasa	Democratic Republic of Congo	One
Libreville	Gabon	Ten
Lome	Togo	One
London	United Kingdom	Ten
Los Angeles	California	Twenty-five
Lyons	Colorado	Four
Malabo	Equatorial Guinea	Two
Memphis	Tennessee	Three
Milwaukee	Wisconsin	Three
Neuss	Germany	Three
New Orleans	Louisiana	Three
New York	New York	Eleven
Olivette	Missouri	Six
Ontario	Canada	Twelve
Orangeburg	South Carolina	Two
Ouagadougou	Burkina Faso	Seven
Paris	France	Eight

Philadelphia	Pennsylvania	Two
Port of Spain	Trinidad and Tobago	Seven
Pretoria	South Africa	Two
Port-au-Prince	Haiti	One
Scotch Plains	New Jersey	Thirteen
Seattle	Washington	Six
Tampa	Florida	One
Toronto	Canada	Two
Washington	District of Columbia	Seventeen
Westport	Connecticut	Two
Yaounde	Cameroon	Eight
Youngstown	Ohio	Two

Table 23: World cities and the Number of Black Women inventors researched

Africa

Figure 4 Map of Africa

Prolific African Innovators and Inventors

Africa, home to almost a billion people, has a rich history and the potential to make a major impression on the world in a variety of ways. It is the birthplace of man and the home of some of the oldest civilizations on Earth – Ancient Egypt (Kamit), Nubia, Kush, Songhai, Ghana, Nok, Igbo-

Ukwu, Mali, Kongo, Yoruba, Benin, the Great Zimbabwe, and the powerful Zulu nation Africans are the inventors of the modern grains consumed by billions of people every day. The image of Africa is often distorted to portray a continent of despair, disease, corruption and disputes. This misrepresentation does no justice to the millions of people from Africa's past and present who have worked hard to document Africa's history and to show that Africa is indeed a continent rich in history, culture and resources.

Africa is a continent filled with mineral wealth. Its land mass can produce more than enough food to feed its growing population. Africa's cultural and historical roots span thousands of years. The descendants of African people who now live in Australia, the Americas, the Caribbean, Europe, Latin America and the South Pacific are awakening to the fact that Africa is their ancestral homeland. We see pieces of Africa displayed in the rhythms of music, the creativity and innovations in hairstyling, artistic displays in clothing and design, awe-inspiring artisanship in furniture and artifacts. Her sons and daughters have set major world records on and off the field, on the courts and in the rings of athletic competition. They have taken the entertainment field by storm; Africa's rhythms now pulsate throughout the world. In the field of science and technology, although little is mentioned about the people of Africa and their descendants, the patents cited earlier are proof of their significant inventions. For more news and information about Africa, visit www.allfrica.com.

African inventors originate from its glorious ancient civilizations as well as its modern day cities and small towns. There are countless inventors from Cameroon, Eritrea, Ethiopia, Ghana, Kenya, Nigeria, and South Africa as well as other countries. Although not all of these inventors now live in their ancestral home, the thousands of patents that they file each year have a significant impact on the world.

African inventors have patented thousands of inventions. September 13th of every year is officially recognized as African Day for Technology and Intellectual Property. On this day, African governments acknowledge the strategic role of technology and intellectual property, a catalyst in the promotion of national development.

African women who have been awarded the World Intellectual Property Organization Gold Medal award are:

Name of Inventor	Description of Invention	Year	Country	Title of Awards
Sebasrienne Adjadobedi	Perfected a process of manufacturing soya flour	2001	Benin	WIPO Gold medal and Diploma
Christine Nare	Process of producing wines from local cereals and fruit	1997	Burkina Faso	WIPO Gold Medal
Group D'initiative Commune de Paysannes de Bogso	Transformation of manioc in bread-making and usable flour in pastry, providing optimum utilization of local nutritional material	2002	Cameroon	WIPO Award
Cecile Kouassi	Process for stabilizing and reconstituting fresh attieke	2000	Cote D'Ivoire	WIPO Gold Medal
Paballo Kibi	Table that can be used as a coffee and or dining table	2001	Lesotho	WIPO Medal
Noromalala Rakotovololona	Sleeping bag	2000	Madagascar	WIPO Gold Medal
Lobo Galle Diallo	Process of manufacturing a powdered extract of ginger	2000	Mali	WIPO Gold Medal
Chrifa Mint Adje	Dietary anti-diarrhea powder	2007	Mauritana	WIPO Gold medal
Nigia Mint Ahmed	Recipe for a marrow (squash) and date preserve	2000	Mauritius	WIPO Gold Medal
Kapinga Mikalu	Mirror-microscope system for saliva test	1990	Zaire	WIPO Gold Medal

Table 24: African women awarded the WIPO Gold Medal or other distinction by country of origin.

African Countries with Black Inventors

Angola

Bernardo Francisco Campos, Luanda, granted a patent for game board, 2002.

[100]

Benin

Achidi Valentin Agon, Cotonou received a patent for an antiviral, anti-infection extract, 2004.

Botswana

Dumisani Itumeleng Anthony Sibiya, Garbarone, co-inventor received a patent for ostomy bag, flushing kit and method, 2004.

Burundi

Libere Ntiunga, Bujumbura, awarded several patents including residential heating and industrial drying technique, 2002.

Burkina Faso

Odile G. Nacoulma, Ouagaougou, co-inventor of extract with anti-tumor and anti-poisonous activity, 2004.

Christine Nare, Ouagaougou, received a patent for alcoholic drinks made from cereals and fruit, 2002.

Cameroon

Tideya Kella, Yaounde, designed and received patents related to radio and wireless telephones, (patents assigned to Infineon Technologies AG), 2001-2005.

Sarah O.E. Ayuk, Yaounde, granted a patent for Calvary soap and its manufacturing process, 2006.

Cape Verde

Joao Baptista Siva Lopes, awarded several patents including low uranium enrichment reactor moderator serving as cooler comprises water heat exchange circuit, with each fuel module cooled individually, 2005.

Central African Republic

Yves Germani, Paris, France, co-inventor received a patent for genetic markers, metabolic markers, and methods for evaluating pathogenicity of strains of e. coli, 2003.

Cesaire Sokambi, Bangui, granted a patent for crank-geared manioc, 2000.

Chad

Guindj Abdoulaye, N'Djamena, received a patent for an enriched flour food called Nigue-Farine, which is particularly beneficial for young children, 1999.

[101]

Congo

Theodore Nzingoula, Brazzaville, granted two patents for a photographic film reader and photographic command operator, 1993.

Cote d'Ivoire

Patrick Bey, Abidjan, awarded a patent for medical tongue depressor containing one or several channels enabling an oxygen supply and other functions, 2007.

Mlle Ouedrago Bintou, Abidjan, earned a patent for a process for making a drink based on red sorrel, 1989.

Democratic Republic of Congo

Clement Muamba Kabasele, Kinshasa, medicines in powder form with an antibiotic effect that cleans the digestive system, the blood, the liver and the kidneys, 1978.

Angel Bilonda, Kinshasa, granted a patent for Bill perfume, 1992.

Equatorial Guinea

Isabel Petra Davies Eiso, Malabo, earned a patent for hands off umbrella, 2004.

Eritrea

Ghirmay Seyoum, Eritrea, co-inventor of inventions related to chemically coated resistant glass (patents assigned to Rohm GMBH), 2002-2004.

Ethiopia

Isaac Ghebre-Sellassie, Ethiopia, received fifteen patents relating to time release, coating and stabilization of drugs, (patents assigned to Warner-Lambert), 1986-2003.

Gabon

Pierre Pyebi-Oyubi, Gabon, received a patent for an intra-abdominal pressure monitoring system, 2006.

Tramini Mado, Libreville, awarded patents for three lotions, "ETAA, Sagina and Afromanunn, 1985.

Gambia

Jamila Ismali, Faraja, awarded several patents including generation and use of dendritic cells, 2003-2004.

Ghana

Kofi Abaka Jackson, Accra, granted a patent for a turbine (patent assigned to Ghana Ministry of Energy and Mines), 1995.

Fred K. Tay, Anloga, received a patent for an accumulated wind and wave power plant, (patent assigned to Council for Scientific and Industrial Research). 2000.

Edward K. Konadu, Ashanti Region, created vaccines against escherichia coli infection, 2000.

Elias Asiam, Kumasi, awarded three patents providing the process for the recovery of noble metals from ore concentrate, 1988-1990.

Guinea

Nema Mathieu Kolie, Conakry, granted a patent for smokehouse appliance for food products, 1996.

Ivory Coast

Kone Dossungui, Cote D'Ivoire, co-inventor received three patents for production of gas from coconut waste or from hevea wood, a gas generator operating on coconut, and a method for extracting manioc (cassava) pulp, by wet and dry means, particularly for preparing manioc (cassava) flour, 1986-1987.

Kenya

Raphael Kollah, Kenya, co-inventor awarded sixteen domestic and foreign patents related to fiberglass coating and sizing (patents are assigned to PPG Industries, Inc., Pittsburgh, PA.), 1998-2003.

Lesotho

Makhaya Mabahle, Maseru, received patent for a curtain rail accessory, 1997.

Liberia

Benjamin F Johnson, Monrovia, granted a patent for a charcoal steam pressing iron, 1995.

Madagascar

Albert Rakoto-Ratsimamnga Antananarivo, developed preparations and therapeutic uses of plants and plant extracts in the hylocereus genus, 2007.

Henry Nrina Rakotomala, Tananarive, developed semi-rotary internal combustion heat engine with double pedal discs 2007.

[103]

Malawi

William Kamkwamba, Malawi, developed and built windmills for electricity out of junkyard parts. 2007.

Peter M. Mashava, Blantyre, granted a patent for isolation of naturally occurring isoflavone and some clinical uses thereof (patents assigned to University of Zimbabwe and Zimbabwe National Traditional Healers Association), 1996.

Mali

Modibo Khan Baradji, Bamako, designed and received a patent for a seasoning cube that is made from tropical products 2003.

Mauritania

Jerome Carcasse, Mauritania inventor won the 1999 Africa awards at the Day of Technology and Intellectual Property, developed an invention that will generate energy from water waves and wind.

Niger

Dr. Hassane Idrissa Souley, Niamey, received a few patents including a natural product against urinary retention and stones, anti-mosquito insecticide by fumigation, and a **secure** electrical plug (Wahab-safe), 1999-2002.

Nigeria

Anthony O. Awesfo, Nigeria, pioneered inventions in the area of paper towels, tissue paper and lotions, (patents assigned to Fort James Corporations, Richmond, VA, 1992-2002.

Olukayode Oluwole, Nigeria, designed a keyboard capable of typing diacritical marks and characters of over four hundred Nigerian languages, 2005

Mohammed Bah Abba, Nigeria, won a $75,000 Rolex Award for Enterprise for his pot-in-pot cooling system, 2001.

Brino Gilbert, Nigeria won two medals and a trophy in May, 2003 at the Invention and New Product Exposition (INPEXP) in the United States. He also won a bronze medal in the Aerospace / Aeronautics category and a silver medal.

Rwanda

Jean de la Croi Habimana, Rwanda, granted a patent for the encapsulation of solar cells, 2005.

Senegal

N'diaye Ousmane Pierre, Senegal, granted two patents for keeping prepared food hot, 1998.

Sierra Leone

Oshoma Momoh, Sierra Leone, received seven patents in computer technology, (patents are assigned to Microsoft), 1999-2002.

South Africa

Carol V. Ndlovu, Capetown, co-inventor created a method of protecting plants against viral infections, 1992.

Zamila Denga, Johannesburg, received six patents for production of organic olefins, production of amides and/or acids from nitriles, separation of linear alpha-olefins from contaminants, removal of oxygenates from a hydrocarbon feed. All patents assigned to Sasol Ind Pty Ltd., 1994-2000.

Phiwayinkosi Gift Mbuyazi, South Africa, received two patents for simulating braided hair and another patent to unravel braided hair, 2000.

Bongani S Nkosi, Sasolburg, co-inventor received six patents concerning metathesis production as well as the production of propylene, (patents were assigned to Sasal Technology Proprietary Limited), 1993-2003.

Humphrey Thulani Dlamini, Vanderbijlpark, co-inventor granted three patents, ferrihydrite and aluminum containing fisher-tropsch catalysts, chemicals from synthesis gas, catalyst (patents assigned to Sasol Technology Proprietary Limited), 2003-2004.

Sudan

Mohammed Al Ameer Sanhory, Khartoum, received a patent for the treatment of cutaneous leishmaniasis and other dermatological diseases, mainly wounds (diabetic ulcers) by idogenos sanhory, 2000.

Tanzania

Theonest K. Mutabingwa Muheza, co-inventor received a patent for malaria vaccines, 2007.

Togo

Kodzovi Agbenowossi Kpomda, Togo, designed and invented two patents related to straps for chin brace and traction cap for vertebral column therapy, 1999-2001.

Uganda

George W. Lubega, Uganda, co-inventor of a vaccination against tyrpanosomiasis, 2003.

[105]

Zambia

Prof. Mulenga Lukwesa Nyamugaba, Zambia received a patent for Tisaniferon, 1994.

Zaire

Kazadi Mabika, Zaire, awarded two patents, including one patent for ultrasonic industrial sorting of diamonds, 1992.

Zimbabwe

Peter M. Mashava, Harare, received a patent for isolation of a naturally occurring isoflavanone and some clinical uses thereof, 1996.

Benson Sibanda, Zimbabwe, awarded five patents related to devices used in the medical field, (patents assigned to Advanced Tissue Sciences, Inc.), 1996-2001.

The list above is a representative sampling of African inventions. The African inventors have been honored for their contributions. The African Union in conjunction with the World Intellectual Property Organization (WIPO) has awarded Africans in the categories of Outstanding Inventor, Woman Inventor, Young inventor and Indigenous Based Technology.

Here is a numerical breakdown of patents held by African countries. Because the research is continuing, the numbers are not conclusive.

African cities and the number of Black inventors researched

City	Country	Number of Patents
Luanda	Angola	One
Cotonou	Benin	Seven
Garbarone,	Botswana	One
Ouagadougou	Burkina Faso	Twenty-six
Bujumbura	Burundi	Four
Yaounde	Cameroon	Seventy-eight
Warwickshire	Cape Verde	One
Bangui	Central African Republic	Two
N'djamena	Chad	Ten
Brazzaville	Congo	Twenty-seven
Abidjan	Cote D'Ivorie	Fifty
Kinshasa	Democratic Republic of Congo	Five
Addis Ababa	Ethiopia	Two
Cairo	Ethiopia	Two
Libreville	Gabon	Fourteen
Farara	Gambia	Two
Accra	Ghana	Twenty-three
Kumasi	Ghana	Twelve
Conakry	Guinea	Twenty-three
Gatundu	Kenya	Two
Nairobi	Kenya	Forty
Maseru	Lesotho	Three
Monrovia	Liberia	Two
Antananarivo	Madagascar	Fifteen
Bamako	Mali	Fifty
Curepipe	Mauritania	Three
Niamey	Niger	Twenty-seven
Abuja	Nigeria	Ten
Ibadan	Nigeria	Four
Ile Ife	Nigeria	Nineteen
Lagos	Nigeria	Thirteen
Owerri	Nigeria	Fifteen
Dakar	Senegal	Twenty-three

Dakar	Senegal	Sixty
Capetown	South Africa	Twenty patents
Johannesburg	South Africa	Fifteen
Sasolburg	South Africa	Six
Khartoum	Sudan	Five
Dar Es Salaam	Tanzania	Ten
Lome	Togo	Twenty-seven
Kampala	Uganda	Eleven
Kinshasa	Zaire	Eight
N'Dola	Zambia	One
Harare	Zimbabwe	Four

Table 25: African Cities and Black inventors

Figure 5 Map of Australia

Prolific Black Inventors from Australia

Australia's Black people have a profound effect on Australia. Like traditional Africans, Chinese, and Native Americans, Australian aborigines use traditional herbs, medicinally. The knowledge and use of the aboriginal traditional medicines has benefitted many people.

David Unaipon, an Aborigine and Australian, was a statesman and inventor. He developed ten inventions, including scissor shears for removing wool from sheep. His image appears on Australia's fifty-

[109]

dollar bill. Unaipon wrote *Legendary Tales of the Australian Aborigine* in which he describes the customs and religious practices of the Aboriginal people.

Aborigines have a deep understanding of mundane and spiritual laws, customs, and tribal laws. They developed a highly evolved and sophisticated system of spirituality, which included knowledge about the Great Spirit. Although there are no books written by the Aborigines of the past, their customs and cultural practices have been passed down orally through generations.

Aborigines developed an initiation system to transform boys and girls into men and women. This system transmitted the knowledge and skills of bush crafts and hunting to young people. They created a way of life that wove myths and folklore together, providing powerful learning tools for their communities

Because of their oral tradition, much of Australian Aborigines' inventiveness has been overlooked. Despite that, there have been some patents granted, particularly to David Unaipon. Below is a small list of patents granted to David Unaipon and three Africans living in Australia.

Australia

David Unaipon, Australia, received a patent for an improvement in sheep shears in 1909.

Robert Kofi Mensah, New South Wales and Orange, received patents related to methods for controlling moths and other insects, 1997-2003.

Anthony Kwaw Quansah, Victoria, received patents for compartment containers and carrying a bag, 1998-1999.

Jonas Addai-Mensah, Mawson Lakes, received two domestic and foreign patents related to scale prevention and removal, 2002-2004.

Figure 6: Map of Canada

Prolific Black Canadian Innovators and Inventors

Black people were brought to Canada as enslaved laborers, or escaped the tyranny of slavery by seeking refuge in Canada, which abolished slavery in 1833. Black people also immigrated to Canada from Africa, the Caribbean, Europe, the United Kingdom and the United States. Some official estimates by the Canadian government show that less than a million Black people live in Canada; however, the impact of the descendants of enslaved Africans has been remarkable. Today, a significant number of African Caribbean, African Americans, Black Australians, Black British and Africans from the continent have immigrated to and made Canada their home. Besides inventors, a number of Black Canadians have had a major impact on Canadian history.

[111]

The first Black person to set foot on Canadian soil was Mathieu Da Costa, a free man who was hired as a translator for Samuel de Champlain's expedition[6]. For more information on Black Canadians, please visit: www.blackhistorycanada.ca.

The Canadian areas with the heaviest concentration of Blacks are Halifax, Montreal, Ottawa and Toronto, but Black inventors hail from practically every province in Canada.

Black Canadians continue to file and receive patents. Research in this area is ongoing.

Name of Inventor	City	Number of Patents
Daniel Boateng	Montrose Ontario	Twenty-eight patents
Patrick Chilufya Chimfwembe, et al.	Derrick, Edmonton	Sixteen patents
Roger E. Gaynor	Oakville, Mississauga.	Fourteen patents
Goodwill M. Igwe	Kingston, Ontario	Eight patents
Juse O. Igweemezie	Markham, Ontario	Five patents
Geraldine Mbamalu	Toronto, Ontario	Two patents

Table 26: Black Canadian Inventors

Alberta

Clarence Medley, Alberta, received a patent for non-refillable bottle, 1907.

Calgary

Ben Ifeanyi Nzekwu, Calgary, received six patents related to well boring and gravity drainage, (patents assigned to Alberta Oil Sand Technology Research and Elan Energy, Inc.), 1995-1997.

Edmonton

Oduditun A. Phillips, Edmonton, received six patents related to medical compositions, (patents assigned to SynPhar Labs), 1997-1999.

Montreal

Charles Kwesi Collinson, Montreal received three patents related to exercise equipment, 1997-2001.

---

[6] Work citied: http://blackhistorycanada.ca/timeline.php?id=1600

Montrose

Daniel D. Boateng, Montrose, received over twenty domestic and foreign patents related to the development of a number of chemical compositions, (patents assigned to Cominco Limited), 1987-1997.

Nova Scotia

Solomon O. Nwaka, Nova Scotia, received five patents related to medical compositions, 2003-2004.

Oakville

Roger E. Gaynor, Oakville, received fifteen patents related to the development of inks, (patents assigned to Xerox), 1995-2004.

Ottawa

Tesfaye Negeria, Ottawa, received a patent for a frothless flotation apparatus, (patent assigned to the Minister of Natural Resources), 1998.

Toronto

Marc Auguste, Toronto, received a patent for a coin and token organizing, holding and dispensing apparatus, 2006.

Modestus Onuora Kay Obochi, Vancouver, received ten domestic and foreign patents for medical compositions for the immune system and prevention of organ transplants rejection (assigned patents to QLT Phototherapeutics, Inc.), 1998-2002.

Weston

Donovan "Razor" Ruddock, Weston, received a patent for a manually operated trash compactor, 2005.

Winnipeg

Tedros Bezebeh, Winnipeg, received two patents, one for the development of antibiotics and a method for identifying a form of cancer, 2003.

Canadian cities and the number of Black inventors researched

City	Province	Number of Patents
Brampton	Ontario	Two
Calgary	Alberta	Thirteen
Cap-de-la-Madeline	Quebec	Two
Derrick	Edmonton	Seven
Edmonton	Alberta	Twelve
Fort McMurray	Alberta	Four
Halifax	Nova Scotia	Five
Kingston	Ontario	Eight
Longueuil	Quebec	Three
Markham	Ontario	Six
Mississauga	Ontario	Two
Montreal	Quebec	Twelve
Montrose	British Columbia	Thirty-five
Oakville	Ontario	Fifteen
Ontario	Ontario	Thirty-one
Ottawa	Ontario	Five
Prince Edward Island	Ontario	One
Quebec City	Quebec	Three
Saskatoon	Saskatchewan	Seven
Toronto	Ontario	Five
Trois-Rivieres-Ouest	Quebec	Four
Vancouver	British Columbia	Fifteen
Victoria	British Columbia	Two
Winnipeg	Manitoba	Five

Table 27: Canadian cities and Black inventors

Figure 7: Map of the Caribbean, Central and South America

Prolific Black Innovators and Inventors from the Caribbean and Central America

The Caribbean islands are home to millions of descendants of Africa. Their enslavement and subsequent forced transplantation to the Caribbean, has led to the mixing of culture and technology. The Caribbean islands are among the most fertile lands on the planet — the island nations are full of mineral wealth as well as a diverse population with various skills and abilities. This has led to the Caribbean islands being among the world leaders not only in entertainment and sports, but also in science and technology. People from the Caribbean have had a major impact on the world of innovation and invention. Despite the foregoing, the focus on the Caribbean is usually on the resorts and the islands' appeal as a vacation paradise. More recognition should be given to Caribbean people who have enlightened the world with their innovations and inventions.

Below are a number of Caribbean inventors who were awarded patents for their ideas and inventions:

Name of Inventor or innovator	Patent or Innovation	Date	Country
Dr. Cardinal Warde	Received fourteen telecommunications related patents	1984-2006	Barbados
David Weeks	Received seven computer related patents	2005-2006	Barbados
Eugene August	A rail joint	1923	Belize
Dugald Clarke	Device for steam to sugar milling	1769	Jamaica
Monique Ennis	System for assisting user with task involving form, and related apparatuses, methods, and computer-readable media	2005	Jamaica
Sybil M Grant	Received patents for swing, jump for music game	2006-2007	Jamaica
Dr. Thomas P. Lecky	Bred three types of cattle suited for Jamaica's environment	1951-1965	Jamaica
Dr. Henry Lowe et al.	Drug from Jamaican plants to treat five types of cancer.	2006	Jamaica
Dr. Sam Street et. al.	Assisted Dr. Lawson Douglas with first kidney transplant performed in Jamaica	1971	Jamaica
Austin J. Thomas	Bred a perch from Africa suited to Jamaica's environment		Jamaica
Dr. Louis Vere	Discovered a number of diseases that had a great impact on the health of Jamaicans		Jamaica
Louis Forde	Received six patents related to engines and the automobile industry	1977-1989	Panama
Dr. Anthony Achong	Has two local patents on the steel pan.		Trinidad & Tobago
Jefferson Cole	Received a patent for a recycling device	2004	Trinidad & Tobago

Stephan Gift	Received a patent for a telephone number verification system and a subscriber pair identification system	1990	Trinidad & Tobago
Buddie Miller	Received patents for slotted hulls for boats and a digital self identification and digital versatile safe card, e-commerce system	2004-2008	Trinidad & Tobago
Dolly Nicholas	Received nine domestic and foreign patents related to trinidad lake asphalt	1999-2005	Trinidad & Tobago
Jacob M. Henriquez	Game board	1882	Venezuela

Table 28: Caribbean and Central American Inventors

Caribbean inventors have filed patents for a significant number of inventions. The influence and scientific discovery of innovators and inventors from the Caribbean has its mark in the annals of inventions. Puerto Rico, acquired over seven hundred domestic and foreign patents between the early 1800's-2007. Cuba, the island nation by itself, is responsible for filing over one thousand five hundred patents from 1920-2007. Caribbean innovators, inventors and scientists have received world recognition and awards.

Antigua

Charles Dumont, St. Johns, received patents for a multidirectional scan, a platform purchase checkout system and a portable self-service bar code marker and reader for purchase monitoring, 1995-1996.

Bahamas

Marcus Matthew, Nassau, developed a design for a wristwatch bracelet, 1949.

James W.M. Skinner, Flatts, received a patent for a leather dressing, 1932.

Barbados

David Weeks. St. Peter, earned seven patents related to global origin and departure information systems and apparatus for securing shipping, 2005-2008.

Carl Wimmer, Christ Church, was granted three patents. These include techniques for creating computer-generated notes, techniques for knowledge discovery by constructing knowledge correlations using concepts or terms, and techniques for magazine-like presentation of advertisement using computers, 2007-2008.

[117]

Bermuda

Clarence Darrell, Flatts, received a design patent for a bicycle pump, 1898.

Cuba

Maurico R. Plancht, Havana, earned seven patents including patents for an auto pump, and explosion motor, improved electric light, improved shipping propeller and pneumatic tube, 1923-1928.

Dominican Republic

Guillermo Solomon Santiago, Santiago, granted patent for an automobile parking device, 1939.

Grenada

Kenrick M Lewis, Grenada, co-inventor received eighteen patents for chemical compositions (patents assigned to Union Carbide Chemicals and Plastics Company Inc. and Witco, Corp), 1986-2006.

Guadeloupe

Rene Le Maigat, Gosier, received a patent for sugar cane field inter-row soil cultivator, 1997.

Guyana

Gregory Onyemauwa Iwu, Georgetown, developed a method of treating bauxite waste, red mud, with acid and making construction bricks from the treated material, 1976.

Haiti

Fenelon Pelissier, Gonaives, received four patents, for a bumper, a placket-closure, and a safety-derailing device, 1907-1912.

Fritz Lolagne, Point-Au-Prince, developed two types of forceps, 1997-1999.

Jamaica

Curtis D. Johnston, Black River, received two patents including a shock absorber and an apparatus for pumping fluids, 1940-1963

Brian Reynolds, Hanover, earned six patents including interactive web book systems, 2000-2006.

Paula Tennent, Kingston, received a patent for papaya ring spot virus genes, 2006.

Sybil B.M. Grant, Mandeville, granted two patents for Jump for Music games and a swing chair, 2006-2007.

Edward Foster, Montego Bay, developed piano strings and frame for same, 1918.

Douglas A. Thompson, St. Ann, granted patent for hydroelectric power plant, 1982.

Martinique

Maurice Hayot, Basse-Pointe, developed a crushing machine for sugar cane stalks, 1965.

Mexico

Lawrence H. Knox, Mexico City, invented over twenty medical products related to steroids, 1961-1969.

Panama

Louis Forde, Panama, received five patents for various engine related inventions, such as the positive electrostatic power system, and rotating ignition, 1978-1990.

Puerto Rico

Jose Capdevila Cucullu, Mayaguez, granted a patent for a process of preserving sugar juices, 1893.

Alono E. Summerville, San Juan, developed a paper clip, 1919.

Santo Domingo

Belisario Silfa, Santo Domingo, developed a spark plug, a puzzle, and a picture frame, 1905-1912.

St. Thomas

Liston Abbott, St. Thomas, received eight patents for a variety of developments that improved television signal capacity. Among them were a means of recovering data from a vestigial sideband of a standard television signal, canceling cross modulation in two color TV signals passed through non-linear path, and a TV piracy system using gray sync, (patents assigned to RCA Corporation and Sanoff Corporation), 1978-2003.

St. Vincent

Leo A. Lewis, St. Vincent, received a patent for an innovative speaker box, 1991.

Trinidad and Tobago

Dr. Anthony Achong, received two patents on the steel pan, 2002.

Chandra Dinnath, Chaguanas, earned a patent for a coconut-husking machine, 1999.

Juliet Lorde, Port of Spain, received a patent for determining and tracking downhole particulate deposition, 2007.

Clarence Augustus Les Phillips, co-inventor, was granted a patent for a desiccant and defoliating spray composition for leguminous plants, 1980.

Venezuela

Sebastian Lacavalerie, Caracas, earned five patents including a patent for a bottle stopper, marine vessel, shell-fuse and a steam generator, 1894-1897.

Caribbean and Central American cities and the number of Black inventor researched:

City	Country	Patents
Nassau	Bahamas	Three
Christ Church	Barbados	Five
St. Peter	Barbados	Seven
St. Thomas	Barbados	Five
Georgetown	Guyana	Two
Gonaives	Haiti	Seven
Port-au-Prince	Haiti	Twenty-seven
Kingston	Jamaica	Fifty
Montego Bay	Jamaica	Four
St. Andrew	Jamaica	Four
Castries	St. Lucia	One
St. Thomas	Virgin Island	Three
Paramaribo	Suriname	Two
Pointe-A-Pierre	Trinidad and Tobago	Thirteen
Port of Spain	Trinidad and Tobago	Twenty
Caracas	Venezuela	Five

Table 29: Black inventors in the Caribbean

Figure 8 Map of Europe

[122]

Prolific Black Innovators and Inventors in Europe

Today, a significant number of Africans live in Europe. Black people from the Diaspora have immigrated to European countries. In addition, Africans were transported to European countries during the Atlantic Slave Trade.

Although an estimated eighteen million Black people now live in European countries, there is very often no mention made of Black inventors located in Europe. In this section, I will list a number of Black inventors and the countries where they have filed their patents.

Black inventors in Europe have patented thousands of inventions. For a number of Black men and women, Europe has served as an alternative to the blighted economic and social conditions in their own countries. Europe has provided educational resources for a number of Black people who now live there. This section of the book highlights some important innovations and inventions developed by the creative genius of Black people from Africa, Canada, the Caribbean, and the United States who live and work in Europe and the United Kingdom.

Name of Inventor or innovator	Number of Patents	Date	Country
Kwaku Frimpong-Ansah et al,	Awarded two patents	1998	Austria
Ukiwo Obasi Onuoha	Received three patents	1997-1999	Switzerland
Dr. Fisseha Merkuria	Received fifteen patents	2000-2006	Sweden
Olukayode Anthony Ojo	Received thirty-eight patents	1993-2004	Netherlands
Benedict O. Olusegun	Developed four patents	1995-1996	France
Derek A. Adeyemi Palmer	Granted nineteen patents	1999-2002	United Kingdom
Ghirmay Seyoum	Received six patents	2002-2004	Germany

Table 30: Black inventors in Europe

[123]

Black inventors in Europe

Austria

Kwaku Frimpong-Ansah, Vienna, co-inventor of a system for transcribing dictation in text files and for revising the text, 2003.

Belgium

Jamila Ismali, Brussels, co-inventor, received a patent for the generation and use of new types of dendritic cells, 2003.

Denmark

Timmi Mensah, Kobenhavn, co-inventor, granted a patent for a cutting device for mounting on a roll of tape, 1997.

Sanya Olufemi, Villigen, developed a method for the sorting of program locations, 1998.

France

Jean-Marie Gueye, La Ciotar, co-inventor, received two patents, developed a method of identifying the owner of a smart card and a display module and chip card using said, 2002.

Meri Etienne, Paris, developed a ginger syrup drink for dilution with water or other ingredients, 1998.

Christophe Luberriaga, Paris, received a patent for an African type electrical string instrument, 1999.

Lucien Maurice, Paris, received a patent for an accumulator of heat, 1899.

Kompany N. K. Tshimamga, Paris, received a patent for his work with wind systems, consisting of primary and secondary systems of wind turbines, transmission shafts and hydraulic turbines, mounted on the same mast to rotate in opposite directions, 2002.

Almadidi Diallo, Thorigne-Foullard, received three patents for a self-regulated synchronous rectifier, DC-DC switching converter, and direct energy converter, (patents assigned to Alcatel and Electro Automatisme Ate), 1990-2002.

Nancy Tidjissa Leo Wouodjiwoua, Paris, developed the extraction of a sapogenin from the trunk of the bedehi plant, and used for medicinal purposes, 1999.

[124]

Germany

Tafadzwa Magaya, Berlin, co-inventor, created a method of electroplating a work piece having high-aspect ratio holes (patent assigned to Atotech Deucthland GMBH), 2004.

Dr. Ermias Dagne, Bonn, co-inventor, developed chemical compounds in isolation and for use in pharmaceutical preparations (patents assigned to Nattermann and Cle, GMBH, Koln), 1985.

Astrid Omoruyi, Dusseldorf, co-inventor, created monomer-poor polyurethane prepolymer, 1998.

Ben Armah, Hamburg, co-inventor, received sixteen patents related to chemical and medical compositions, (patents assigned to Beirsdorf Aktiengesellchaft), 1982-2002.

Benjamin Mbouombouo, Munich, co-inventor, developed a method of providing clock signals to load circuits in an ASIC device, (patent assigned to LSI Logic Corporation), 2001.

Tideya Kella, Munchen, co-inventor, received ten patents related to radiotelephones, mobile telephone equipment, (patents assigned to Infineon Technologies AG), 2001-2002.

Gerard Georges, Wolfsburg, co-inventor, received fifteen patents for innovative automotive designs for brakes, engines, and spark insertions, among others, (patents assigned to Volkswagenwerk Aktiengesellschaft), 1973-1979.

Italy

Akililu Lemma, Florence, developed a method of controlling zebra mussels, 1994.

Toudie Roger Gbohou, Pardova, created a new bank/market organizational model, 2001.

Mathias Christian Zohoungbogbo, Torino, granted a patent for a pharmaceutical composition for treating side effects of a diet with reduced amount of carbohydrates, 1999.

Netherlands

Gebre Admasu, Amersfoort, co-inventor, received four patents for a vehicle guidance system, a traffic management, and an electronic payment parking lot system, 1992-2002.

Kofi Afolabi A. Makinwa, Eindhoven, co-inventor, received over twenty patents related to computer equipment including hard drives, pen

[125]

detection, personal data assistant (PDA), and touch computer screens among others (patents assigned to U.S. Phillips, and Phillips Electronics), 1995-2003.

Olukayode Anthony Ojo, Eindhoven, co-inventor, received a number of patents related to picture signals, noise reduction and video signal processing, (patents assigned to Phillips Electronics, U.S. Phillips Corp.), 1993-2004.

Poland

Kenneth Ogbonna Udeh received three patents related to medical compositions, 1999-2003.

Slovenia

Adama Toure, Maribor, granted two patents for combined warm water furnace and a water heater, 1994-1995.

Spain

Tesfamariam Yosief, Tres Contos, co-inventor, developed cytotoxic alkaloid derivatives including asmarine A and B isolated from a sponge, (patent assigned to Institute Bomar), 2002.

Sweden

Dr. Fisseha Mekuria, Lund, co-inventor, received twenty patents related to cell phone technology including: voice dialing, communication device, images, voice recognition and text to speech among others, (patents assigned to Ericsson Telefon AB L M), 2000-2006.

Samuel Gebre-Medhin, Goteborg, co-inventor, received patent for transgenic animals with recombinant vascular endothelial growth factor b (vegf-b) DNA and uses thereof, 2001.

Alaiya Ayodele, Stockholm, received two patents for materials and methods relating to disease diagnosis, 2000-2001.

Switzerland

Nwaeze Anyanwu, Geneva, developed a process for determining 17-ketosteroids in urine and blood and solutions for carrying out this process, 1970.

Fall Mbaye, Schliem, received patents for an AC/DC voltage converter and switching power supply with a snubber circuit, 1999-2003.

Ukiwo Obasi Onuoha, Zurich, co-inventor, received three patents for flame-retardant and water sellable polyurethane compositions 1997-1999.

Ukraine

Franc Ovusu, Khakiv, received two patents for surgical procedures developed to treat spleen damage, 2007.

European Cities and the Number of Black Inventors Researched

City	Country	Patents
Vienna	Austria	Three
Brussels	Belgium	Five
Copenhagen	Denmark	Three
Les Ulis	France	Eight
Paris	France	One Hundred
Berlin	Germany	Six
Eglesbach	Germany	Eight
Munchen	Germany	Ten
Hamburg	Germany	Fifteen
Munchen	Germany	Ten
Wolfsburg	Germany	Fourteen
Torino	Italy	Three
Eindhoven	Netherlands	Seventy-Two
Barcelona	Spain	Three
Lund	Sweden	Eighteen
Stockholm	Sweden	Three
Uppsala	Sweden	Five
Geneva	Switzerland	Seventeen
Khakiv	Ukraine	Three

Table 31: Black inventors in European cities

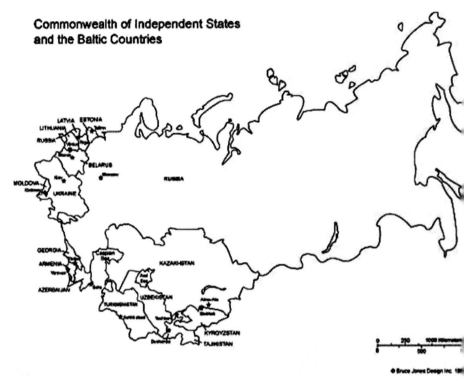

Commonwealth of Independent States
and the Baltic Countries

Figure 9 Map of Russia

Black Inventors in Russia

Black influence in Russia can be traced back to Africa. Over the years, more than four hundred thousand Africans have migrated to Eastern Europe and Russia to take advantage of educational opportunities. Below are a few of the Black inventors who were awarded patents for their ideas and inventions:

Ogigure Obofoni Dzouzef, Russia, co-inventor, developed a method of producing aggregate for concrete mix and initial composition for producing white cement clinker, 1990-1995.

Dossu-Iovo, P Er, Russia, co-inventor, received three patents related to production of small balls of fish base and fish cutlets, 2002-2003.

Andres Michi Ndong, Russia, co-inventor, received two patents for a method for manufacture of fishing gear and fish trawling method 1994-1995.

[128]

Figure 10 Map of the United Kingdom

[129]

Black inventors in the United Kingdom

Blacks in Britain can trace their roots back to Africa. Britain was heavily involved in the slave trade and benefited tremendously from the trade and enslavement of Africans (White). Black labor has been the backbone of British economic growth. British Blacks currently represent approximately one percent of the population or an estimated one million Black people.

The focus of this section is the tremendous intellectual, innovative, and inventive impact Black inventors in Britain have had on their country. For more information on the Black presence in Britain, visit:
http://www.black-history-month.co.uk
http://www.blackpresence.co.uk.

Collectively Black inventors in the United Kingdom have thousands of inventions in all fields of technology. The following pages contain the names of a number of Black inventors who were awarded patents for their ideas and inventions:

Arvans
Paul Kaine, Arvans, received three patents related to signal monitoring, telephone apparatus and test apparatus, 2001-2002.

Bedford
Adeola Florence Ojo, Bedford, received patents for removal of carbon dioxide from gas streams and zeolites and their use in the separation of nitrogen from other gases, 1995-1997.

Bedfordshire
Joshua Nee Adjah Okunor, Bedfordshire, granted a number of patents related to power tools, (patents assigned to Desoutter Limited), 1982-1991.

Birmingham
Washington Odur Ayuko, Birmingham, awarded patents for medicaments and diagnostic devices, 1994-1995.

Caline

Ademola O. Akinmade, Caline, co-inventor, received patents for dental cements, hydrogel material, and base reaction cements, (patents assigned to BTG, Ltd), 1993-2000.

Cheshire

Raymond Coleman, Cheshire, received two patents for testing electrical equipment and transformer testing, (patents assigned to Era Patents Ltd.), 1988.

Copthorne

Godfrey Henry Oliver Palmer, Copthorne, received two patents for malting process, (patents assigned to Brewing Patents Limited), 1973-1975.

Edinburgh

Abraha Habtemariam, Edinburgh, co-inventor, received two patents for ruthenium anticancer complexes and ruthenium (II) complexes for the treatment of tumors, 2004.

Essex

Joseph Olajibu, Essex, co-inventor, received five patents for dynamic protection bandwidth allocation in BLSR networks and method of deactivating working fiber resources in optical ring networks, among others, (patents assigned to Nortel Networks Limited), 1997-2003.

London

Jacob Kwaku Boateng, London, received fifteen patents for Serverplus, teaching aids, exchangless universal radiophone and telephones, 1984-2000.

Farnborough

Derek Adeyemi Palmer, Farnborough, co-inventor, granted fourteen domestic and international patents including method and apparatus for chemical synthesis (patents assigned to Kalibrant Limited), 1999-2002.

Liverpool

Leslie J. Burrage, Liverpool, co-inventor, received four patents including separation of gamma benzene hexachloride, (patents assigned to Imperial Chemical industries Limited), 1950-1954.

Surrey

Kunle Onabolu, Surrey, awarded five patents including concrete building products, 1993-1996.

Scotland

Bearsden

Eric Aboagye, Bearsden, received a patent for fluorinated 2-nitroimidazole analogs for detecting hypoxic tumor cells, 1998.

Glasgow

Oluyinka A. Awojobi, Glasgow, awarded a patent for radiation measuring and integrating device, 1971.

United Kingdom Cities and the Number of Black Inventors Researched

City	Country	Patents
Bearsden	Scotland	One
Bedford	United Kingdom	Seven
Berkshire	United Kingdom	Six
Birmingham	United Kingdom	Twelve
Bristol	United Kingdom	One
Buckinghamshire	United Kingdom	Two
Caline	United Kingdom	Twelve
Cardiff	United Kingdom	Nine
Cambridge	United Kingdom	Six
Cobham	United kingdom	Six
Edinburgh	United Kingdom	Three
Essex	United Kingdom	Sixteen
Farnborough	United Kingdom	Eighteen
Glasgow	United Kingdom	Nine
Hayes	United Kingdom	Eight
Lancashire	United Kingdom	Nine
Leicester	United Kingdom	Eleven

[132]

Liverpool	United Kingdom	Twelve
London	United Kingdom	One hundred eighty
Manchester	United Kingdom	Five
Middlesex	United Kingdom	Eleven
Oldham Lancashire	United Kingdom	Seven
Oxford	United Kingdom	Six
Staffordshire	United Kingdom	Ten
Surrey	United Kingdom	Fifteen
Witney	United Kingdom	Seven

**Table 32: United Kingdom Cities and the Number of Black Inventors'
Researched**

Design Patents Awarded to Black Inventors

In the world of design patents, Black inventors have left their indelible mark. Their designs range from the very simple to the extremely complex:

Name of Inventor	Invention	Date	City
Christopher Aire	Received three patents for watches	2003-2005	Los Angeles, California
Donald Samuels	Received ten patents for toys	1980-1983	Warwick, Rhode Island
Samuel A. Awei	Granted three patents for toys	1998-2002	Philadelphia, Pennsylvania
Ndukwe Akwiwu	Awarded patents for luminous remote controls	1997	London, United Kingdom
Pedro M. Alfonso	Granted fourteen patents for computer desks, computer cabinets and pen based computers among other inventions	1988-2001	Austin, Texas
Kofi Bissah	Granted seven patents related to pattern absorbent article	2000-2003	Somerset, New Jersey
Felix M. Batts	Smoke gun	1995	Wilson, North Carolina
Saheed Oluwase Fawehinmi	Developed exterior surface of a pair of automobile doors, and automobile body	1997	Lanham, Maryland,
Edward T. Welburn	Vehicle body	1987	Detroit, Michigan
Sally E. Thimm-Kelly	Combined splint holder and wrist holder	1988	Irving, Texas
Paul E. Johnson	Developed seven therapeutic lamps	1928-1932	Chicago, Illinois
Abbasali A. Currimjee	Chair	1992	Port Louis, Mauritania
Chidi Okonkwo	Created eleven car and truck designs	2000-2004	Atlanta, Georgia,
Juliana M. Puckerin	Wall-hanging toilet paper holder	1998	Port of Spain, Trinidad and

			Tobago
John P. Amoah	Shoe	1994	Brentwood, New York
Vincent L. Haley	Soap Dish	1996	Orrville, Ohio
Wilson W. Smith III	Granted over seventy patents for athletic shoes	1992-2006	Tualatin, Oregon,
Darrell Clarence	Bicycle pump	1898	Flatts, Bahamas
Richard W.E. Willis	Game board or similar article	1959	Kingston, Jamaica
Stella St. John	Umbrella boot holder	1986	Christ Church, Barbados
Odudotun A. Phillips	Novel penam sulfones as beta-lactmase inhibitors	1998	Edmonton, Canada
Brenda M.W. Kahari	Necklace	1994	Harare, Zimbabwe

Table 33: Black inventors and their design patents

Trademarks of Black Innovators and Inventors

Black innovators and inventors have sought the right to protect their intellectual property and products through trademarks. Trademarks are classified as "live" or dead", and are generally valid for ten years.

What are trademarks ? A trademark is denoted as a:

> word, letter, device, sound or symbol or some combinations of these that is used in connection with merchandise, distinctly points inherently or by association to the not necessarily known origin or ownership of that to which it is applied, and is legally reserved to the exclusive use of the owner according to statutory provisions: a name or symbol used by a maker or seller to identify distinctively his products <must display his ~ on his product for it to be legally valid >

The following innovative Black entrepreneurs collectively have over three hundred trademarks, making their combined business worth over two billion dollars.

Cathy L. Hughes, Omaha, Nebraska, currently owns sixteen trademarks on her TV-One Television Production company and has held over forty trademarks with her Radio One, Inc.

Robert L. Johnson, Hickory, Mississippi, former CEO of Black Entertainment Television has over sixty-six trademarks assigned to his former company. He is a successful part owner of the Charlotte Bobcats

Tom Joyner™, Tuskegee, Alabama, has twelve trademarks, including his name, a nationally syndicated radio show and highly successful television show on TV One™.

Oprah Winfrey™, born in Kosciusko, Mississippi, has over sixty-one trademarks.

Name City, State, Country	Trademark Names:	Trademarks Live or Dead
Oprah Winfrey™ Kosciusko, MS.	Harpo Productions; O The Oprah Magazine; The Oprah Winfrey Show; O Oprah Winfrey Scholars; Oprah's 21st Century Schools; Oprah's 21st Century Learning Center; Oprah Winfrey's Legends Ball; Harpo; Oprah; Get Movin' With Oprah; Keep Movin' With Oprah; Ten Steps To A Better Body; Oprah's Book Club; Remembering Your Spirit; Use Your Life; Live Your Best Life; Oprah's Angel Network; The Womankindness Project; Oprah's Womankindness Project; Dr. Phil.; At Home; Oprah's Favorite Things; Oprah's Pop Star Challenge; In Your Wildest Dreams With Oprah; Wildest Dreams With Oprah; Oprah's Kindness Revolution; Inside The Lives	66
Cathy L. Hughes Omaha, NE.	TV-One 1 Television Productions Inc.; TV-One; I See Black People; I Hear Black People; G. Garvin; The Road Tour; Radio One; Code One; Myone; IMC Indy's Music Channel; Interactive Hip Hop & R&B; The People's Expo; Up Close And Personal; Unity Through Music; African American Cultural Festival; Check Yourself; The Station That Plays The Hits the Station That Jams The Most Music; Stone Soul Picnic	58
Russell Simmons™ Queens, NY.	Russell Simmons Argyle Culture; American Classics by Russell Simmons; Def Poets; Russell Simmons; If It Doesn't Say Russell Simmons; It's not Premium; Premium Collection By Russell Simmons; Russell Simmons Def Poetry; Russell Simmons Def Poetry Jam On Broadway; Rush Communications; Get Your House In Order; Russell Simmons Music Group; Rsmg Russell Simmons Music Group; S Simmons Jewelry Co.; Energize; Empower; Excel,	34
Byron E. Lewis Newark, NJ.	Uniworld; Urban Force; Uniworld Group; Unimundo	13
Tyra Banks™ Inglewood, CA.	Tyra Banks; Tzone; Classy Catcher	24
Kimora Lee ™, St. Louis, MO.	Imora; Ming Lee Soul Café; Kimora Lee; Aoki Lee Simmons; Ming Lee Simmons; KLS; Kimora Lee Simmons; Kimora Lee; Fabulosity; KLS Kimora Lee Simmons; Kimora; Simmons Jewelry Company,	81
Clarence O. Smith Bronx, NY.	Essence; Tresessence; Essence Style; Essence By Mail; Essence Art; Essence Award; Essencease; Essence Books For Children; Essence Music Festival; Essence Marketplace; Ebm; Salon Network By Essence; Suede; Take Back The Music	30
Kanye West™ Atlanta, GA.	Kanye West; Mascotte by Kanye West; Kanye West's Glow in the Dark	27

Name City, State, Country	Trademark Names:	Trademarks Live or Dead
John H. Johnson Arkansas City, AR. .	Ebony; Jet, Raveen; Duke; Jack And Jill; Luxury I Press; Easy To Comb; Black World; Mama Write- On's Scribblin' Scope; Vita-Gro; Black Stars; Fashion Fair; Miss Ebony; Mr. J.; Sunny And Honey; Ebony Fashion Fair; Shades Of Fantasy; Polish Perfect; Ebony Man; Ebone; Em; Vantex; Cover Tone; Relaxer Plus; American Black Achievement Awards; Another Fine Product From Ebony; Rap Radio Wjpc; Dazzle; Breathless; Ebony E Style Spiegel; Zahra; Hidden Beauty Skin Enhancing Crème; Jet Quest; Black Family Reunion Celebration; Ebony Black Family Reunion Tour; Jet Quest; Fashion Fair It's You; Fast Finish; Hollywood In Harlem; Ebony Living; Ebony Home	98
Robert L. Johnson Hickory, MS.	BET; The Urban Contemporary Channel; Black Entertainment Television; Jazz Central; Video Soul; Rap City; Live From L.A.; Teen Summit*; BET Productions; Young Sisters & Brothers; Emerge; BET On Music; Your Music Store On The Air; BET On Learning; Rabesque; Video Lp; Personal Diary; Comic view; BET's Listening Party; Bunky; BET Shop; BET.Com; Caribbean Rhythms; Heart & Soul; BET Soundstage Restaurant; BET networks; Where Music Lives; BET Books; Midnight Love; Hits From The Street; Jazz Scene; BET Music Publishing; The BET Video Collection; Backstage Gear; BET Backstage Gear; BET Kid; BET Kids; BET On Wheels; BET On Jazz International; BET Tonight; Jam Zone; BET International; Planet Groove; BET On Jazz The Jazz Channel; The Heart And Soul Exclusive Spa Tour; Latin Beat; Black Star Power; BET Uptown	30 BET Holdings, 358 (BET) Black Entertainment Television
Tom Joyner Tuskegee, AL.	Go With The Bit; Tom Joyner Sky Show TV; Tom Joyner Sky; Tom Joyner Sky Show; The Tom Joyner Morning Show; Tom Joyner's Right Back At'cha; The Tom Joyner Family Reunion; Fantastic Voyage; The Tom Joyner Foundation Flyjock; Tom Joyner's "On The Move"	12
Earl G. Graves Brooklyn, NY.	Black Enterprise; Powerplay; Moneywise; Teenpreneurs; Sistersinc; Black Enterprise For Teens; Black Enterprise For Teens3; Black Enterprise Unlimited; Newspoints; Postscript Kidpreneur News; B.E. For Kids; Kidpreneur; B.E. 100s; B.E.; B.E. Board Of Economists; Black Enterprise; Verve	45
Corretta Scott King, Heiberger, Alabama,	"First Lady of the Civil Rights Movement"	1

Name City; State; Country	Trademark Names:	Trademarks Live or Dead
Rosa Parks Tuskegee, Alabama	Eight listed including; named streets; boulevards and drives	8
Nelson Mandela™ Mvezo; near Mthatha; Eastern Cape; South Africa	Nelson Mandela, Champion Of Freedom Nelson Mandela 1962-1990; Nelson Mandela Children's Fund, Nelson Mandela Educational Trust, The Mandela Freedom Museum; Nelson Mandela Bay Emerging Entrepreneur's Forum, Nelson Mandela Aventis Project For Combating TB; Mandela Walk To Freedom Tours, Nelson Mandela Metropolitan Music Association together Nelson Mandela Co-Operative Ltd	18
Winnie Mandela Bizana, Pondoland, Eastern Cape Province	Winnie Mandela Family Museum	1
Percy E. Sutton San Antonio, TX.	Quics; It's Showtime At The Apollo; Street Literacy Clinic "The Magic Of Learning"; Apollo The World Famous Apollo Theatre Presents Apollo Theatre Records; Apollo The World Famous Apollo Theatre Presents Apollo Theatre Home Video; Apollo The World Famous Apollo Theatre Presents Apollo Theatre Entertainment; Apollo The World Famous Apollo Theatre Presents Amateur Night At The Apollo; Apollo The World Famous Apollo Theatre Presents Apollo Theatre Music Publishing; Apollo The World Famous Apollo Theatre Presents Apollo Entertainment Television; Inner City Films A Division Of Inner City Broadcasting Corp.; Apollo The World Famous Apollo Theatre Presents Apollo All-Star Rhythm & Blues Revue	16
Dr. Martin Luther King Atlanta, Georgia	Over nine hundred named streets; drives and Boulevards. Celebrating The Life; Work And Legacy Of Dr. Martin Luther King; Jr.; Dr. Martin Luther King; Jr. Holiday Breakfast Celebration; In The Footsteps Of Dr. King Award; Martin Luther King, Jr. Community Choir San Diego; Martin Luther King; Jr.; Martin Luther King, Jr.; The King Center; Only African American to have a National Holiday in the United States	908
Malcolm X™ Shabazz; North Omaha, Nebraska	Over One hundred thirty listed; with a number of named streets; drives and boulevards; Malcolm X; X	130
Harriet Tubman (Dorchester County, Maryland)	Harriet Tubman; Harriet Tubman Foundation	2
Frederick Douglass (Talbot County, Maryland)	Eight listings including named streets; drives and boulevards including a United States postage stamp	8

Name City, State, Country	Trademark Names:	Trademarks Live or Dead
Marcus Garvey St. Ann Bay, St. Ann Parish, Jamaica	Six listings including named drives and boulevards including Marcus Garvey Drive, Kingston, Jamaica	6
Dr. George Washington Carver™ Diamond, Missouri	Six listings including Dr. George Washington Carver, Dr. George Washington Carver Prize; Dr. George Washington Carver United States postage stamp	6
Dr. Charles R. Drew Washington, DC.	Charles R. Drew University of Medicines and Science	1
Medgar Evers Decatur, Mississippi	Listed streets including Medgar Evers Institute; Medgar Evers College; Medgar Evers Library	2
Jomo Kenyatta Ichaweri, Gatundu, Kenya	Kenyatta Drive; Nairobi; Kenya; Jomo Kenyatta International Airport	4

Table 34: Important Black men and women and their trademarks

Michael Baisden™, Chicago, Illinois, has developed a number of unique radio programs that bring many issues in the Black community to the forefront. His national syndicated radio program "Love, Lust and Lies™" is particularly popular. Baisden has also developed a number of trademarked radio programs including "The Michael Baisden Show™", "The Naughty Boys™", "The Baisden Beauty™", "Everything is Everything™", "Happily Single™", and "Mingle City™"; through his company, Baisden Enterprise Inc.

Tony Brown, Charleston, West Virginia, founded Tony Brown Productions and "The Tony Brown Journal", one of the longest running programs on PBS. Mr. Brown was one of the first to address a number of hard-hitting issues in the Black community. His award-winning programs gave the Black community a venue for viewing issues and developments of concern to the Black community. Tony Brown has three trademarks The Library of Black History™, The Freedom Seal Buy Freedom $™; Tony Brown Online the Empowerment Network™.

Imhotep Gary Byrd, Buffalo, New York, has been involved in the radio business for over forty years, as a poet, radio griot, and composer. Imhotep Gary Byrd has developed a unique approach to music, interviews and informative radio shows. He has dealt with a number of issues affecting not only Black people in the United States, but also issues that have a global

[140]

perspective. Byrd is responsible for a number of innovative programs, including: "The Gary Byrd Experience", "Radio Theater of the Mind", "Global Black Experience", "Global Beat Experience", and the "GBE Radio Network". Byrd has also authored a song, The Crown.

Tavis Smiley™, Gulfport, Mississippi, radio and television host has developed a variety of radio and television shows through trademarked programming: "Covenant With Black America™", "State of The Black Union™"; "Tavis™" "Youth To Leaders™", "Tavis Smiley™, "Tavis Smiley Presents™".

Barbara Smith "B. Smith", Western Pennsylvania, fashion model, restaurateur, television host, author. Ms. Smith, currently hosts her own show, "B. Smith with Style™", and has eight trademarks. Among her trademarks are B. Smith with Style Home collection™; B. Smith Town & Country Jewelry Collection™; B. Smith Furniture Collection™. In addition, B. Smith is the spokeswoman for Colgate Palmolive Oxy Plus dishwashing liquid and is the new face for the Betty Crocker Cornbread and Muffin Mix.

Black Innovators in Sports and their Trademarks

Black people have played a significant role in the creation and development of exercise equipment, games and toys. Every athlete who plays professional sports should consider trade marking his or her name. A trademark can attract commercial endorsements and provide a financial vehicle to ensure economic stability for the athlete and his or her family. Athletes become public icons and this status transforms them into household names around the world.

Muhammad Ali™, Louisville, Kentucky, a three-time heavyweight champion and Olympic Champion, has ten trademarks and recently sold the rights to the use of his name for fifty million dollars. George Foreman™, Houston, Texas, a two time Heavyweight Champion and Olympic Champion, has eighteen trademarks. John Arthur "Jack" Johnson, (Jack Johnson) Galveston, Texas, the world's first Black Heavyweight Boxing Champion of the world was awarded two patents.

The late Arthur Ashe™, Richmond, Virginia, won three Grand Slams. There are ten trademarks associated with his name.

Billy Blanks, Erie, Pennsylvania, martial arts champion, actor and exercise instructor started an exercise trend in the 1990's called "Tae Bo™". Billy Blanks has thirteen trademarks in the workout fitness arena.

Michael Jordan™, Brooklyn, New York, six times NBA World Champion, and Olympic Champion and a future Hall of Famer. Michael Jordan, perhaps the greatest sports and marketing icon, has over twenty trademarks and his name has generated over one billion dollars in revenue. Ervin "Magic" Johnson™, Lansing, Michigan, six times NBA World Champion and Olympic Champion has over thirty trademarks. Shaquille O'Neal™, Newark, New Jersey four time NBA World Champion and Olympic Champion has twenty-nine trademarks to his name and owns his own-trademarked company. Lebron James™, Akron, Ohio, has received nineteen trademarks and has been dubbed the next Michael Jordan™. Dwayne Wade™, Chicago, Illinois, 2006 NBA World Champion and Most Valuable Player in the 2006 NBA World Championship Series has four trademarks.

Carl Lewis™ Birmingham, Alabama, four-time track and field Olympic Champion of the 100 meters, 200 meters, four by four 100 meters, and long jump championships, has one trademark. The late and great Jessie Owens™, Danville, Alabama, has seven trademarks associated with his name. Mr. Owens won four-gold medals in the 1936, Olympics in Berlin, Germany, and has eight trademarks. The late Florence "Flojo" Griffith Joyner™, Los Angeles, California, won seven Olympic medals, four gold medals and three silver medals. FloJo also won a gold and silver medal at the 1987 Rome World Championship. She had seven trademarks. Jackie Joyner Kersee™, East St. Louis, Missouri, won a silver medal in 1984 Olympics two gold medals at the 1988 Olympics, a gold medal in the 1992 Olympics, and a bronze medal in the 1996 Olympics. She has seven trademarks associated with her name.

Edson Arantes do Nascimento "Pele™", Tres Coracoes, Brazil. This Brazilian international soccer champion, acclaimed King of Football and winner of three World Cups has seventeen trademarks to his name.

The late Eddie Robinson™, Jackson, Louisiana, Grambling University coach. With over four hundred college wins, Mr. Robinson has sent hundreds of Black football players to the National Football League, Canadian Football League, the former American Football and World Football Leagues. His coaching style emphasized principles designed to cultivate responsible men, not just good athletes and football players. Coach Robinson was a great coach, and mentor to his players. Mr. Robinson had one trademark in his name.

The late Walter Payton™, Columbia, Mississippi, key player in the 1984 Super Bowl Championship, who at one-time held the record for rushing yards in the National Football League (NFL). Vince Young™ Houston, Texas, one trademark, Bo Jackson™, Bessemer, Alabama, eight trademarks, Jerry Rice™, Crawford, Mississippi, three trademarks, Donavan McNabb™, Chicago, Illinois, two trademarks, Franco Harris™, Fort Dix, New Jersey, two trademarks, Emmitt Smith™, Pensacola, FL., eleven trademarks, Steve McNair™, Mount Olive, Mississippi, four trademarks. These players have all transformed the college and professional game of football.

Hank Aaron™, Mobile, Alabama, two trademarks, Willie Mays™, Westfield, Alabama, three trademarks, Jackie Robinson™, Cairo, Georgia, six trademarks. These athletes have forever left their mark on Major League Baseball (MLB) and have all been inducted into the National Baseball Hall of Fame. Barry Bonds™, Riverside, California, has one trademark.

Venus Williams™, Saginaw, Michigan, and Serena Williams™, Linwood, California, have won all of the coveted tennis championships including the Australian Open, the French Open, Wimbledon and the US Open championships. They have earned over thirty-five millions dollars in tournament prize money. The Williams sisters have seven trademarks to their names.

Tiger Woods™, Cypress, California, has won seventy-seventy golf tournaments, including the Masters Golf championships four times, earned over ninety million dollars and has twenty-one trademarks associated to his name.

Team owners and advertisers have reaped astronomical profits from the efforts of these talented athletes.

Black Innovators in the Video Game Industry

In 2004, the video game industry generated over ten billion dollars in revenue, which is more money than Hollywood makes from releasing its blockbuster movies. Black game designers are now a crucial part of this multi-billion dollar business. Below is a list of Black game designers and some of the games they ably assisted in designing.

Todd Quincey Jefferson, an African American video game producer, employed by Activision in Santa Monica, California, has worked on more than twenty titles. His name is associated with the trademarks on the following titles:

Video Game Title	Developer	Year
Disney Friends	Disney Interactive Studios	2007
Marvel Ultimate Alliance	Activision Publishing, Inc	2006
X-Men: The Official Game	Activision Publishing, Inc	2005
Shrek SuperSlam	Activision Publishing, Inc	2005
Ultimate Spider-Man (Limited Edition)	Activision Publishing, Inc	2005
X-Men Legends II: Rise of Apocalypse	Activision Publishing, Inc	2005
Lemony Snicket's A Series of Unfortunate Events	Activision Publishing, Inc	2004
Pitfall: The Lost Expedition	Activision Publishing, Inc	2004
Pitfall: The Lost Expedition	Activision Deutschland GmbH	2004
Shrek 2	Activision Publishing, Inc	2004
Shrek 2: Beg for Mercy!	Activision Publishing, Inc	2004
Spider-Man 2	Activision Publishing, Inc	2004
X-Men: Legends	Activision Publishing, Inc	2004
Tony Hawk's Underground	Activision Publishing, Inc	2003
True Crime: Streets of LA	Activision Publishing, Inc	2003
X2: Wolverine's Revenge	Activision Publishing, Inc	2003
Blade II	Activision Publishing, Inc	2002
Spider-Man: The Movie	Activision Publishing, Inc	2002
X-Men: Next Dimension	Activision Publishing, Inc	2002
Disney's The Lion King: Simba's Mighty Adventure	Activision Publishing, Inc	2001
Mat Hoffman's Pro BMX	Activision Publishing, Inc	2001
Spider-Man 2: Enter Electro	Activision Publishing, Inc	2001
Spider-Man 2: The Sinister Six	Activision Publishing, Inc	2001
Spider-Man: Mysterio's Menace	Activision Publishing, Inc	2001

[145]

Tony Hawk's Pro Skater 2	Activision Publishing, Inc	2001
Tony Hawk's Pro Skater 3	Activision Publishing, Inc	2001
X-Men: Reign of Apocalypse	Activision Publishing, Inc	2001
X-Men: Wolverine's Rage	Activision Publishing, Inc	2001
Road Champs: BXS Stunt Biking	Activision Publishing, Inc	2000
Spider-Man	Activision Publishing, Inc	2000
Star Trek: Armada	Activision, Inc	2000
Vigilante 8: Second Offense	Activision Publishing, Inc	2000
X-Men: Mutant Academy	Activision Publishing, Inc	2000
Space Invaders	Activision, Inc.	1999
Asteroids	Activision, Inc.	1998
Battlezone	Activision, Inc.	1998
Dark Reign: Rise of the Shadowhand	Activision, Inc.	1998
Tenchu: Stealth Assassins	SMEI	1998
Dark Reign: The Future of War	Activision Publishing, Inc.	1997
Heavy Gear	Activision, Inc.	1997

Table 35: Video games developed with input of Todd Q. Jefferson (1997-2007)

Rob Gatson, software engineer of Visual Concepts, has written the programming code for several video games. Mr. Gatson joined Visual Concepts in 2001.

Video Game Title	Developer	Year
NBA 2K2	Visual Concepts	2002
NBA 2K3	Visual Concepts	2003
ESPN NBA 2K4	Visual Concepts	2004
ESPN NBA 2K5	Visual Concepts	2005
NBA 2K6	Visual Concepts	2006

Table 36: Video games developed with the input of Rob Gatson

Joseph Saulter, CEO of Entertainment Arts Research has developed a number of video games.

Video Game Title	Developer	Year
Kaotic Foolz	Entertainment Arts Research	
Billy Zane	Entertainment Arts Research	
Whazz Up	Entertainment Arts Research	
Girlz Brawl	Entertainment Arts Research	
Kenji Kenju	Entertainment Arts Research	
Seventh Day	Entertainment Arts Research	

Table 37: Video Games developed by Joseph Saulter

Black innovators in the Music Industry

...African survivals exist not merely in the sense the African American music has the same characteristics as its African counterparts, but also that the musical tendencies, the mythological beliefs and assumptions, and the interpretative strategies of African Americans are the same as those that underlie the music of the African homeland, that these tendencies and beliefs continue to exist as African cultural memory, and that they continue to inform the continuity and elaboration of African American music[7]

Songs, rhythms and compositional arrangements are all tied into the success of the music industry. It is an incontrovertible fact that Black people have had a tremendous impact on music throughout the world. The Ancient Egyptians first explored and came to understand the interrelationship between rhythms, minerals, plants, animals, people and God, through their deity Het Heru[8]. This deity governs rhythm, instruments, dance, art and music. Het Heru is also responsible for creative visualization and the imagination (inventions, wealth, and fertility) as well as all social harmony and interactions between people, nations, and nature. This deity and its interrelationship to humankind was recognized, developed, cultivated, and expressed in all the world's continents. Het Heru is known by many different names. To the Yoruba of West Africa she is Oshun, in Brazil she is known as Marimba, and in Roman mythology, she is called Venus.

Inventors and innovators are dreamers. It is this imaginative function that allows them to visualize the ideas they want to create. These ideas materialize as their inventions. Blues, gospel, jazz, rhythm and blues, soul, and funk all originated in the Black community. A number of Black performers, over the years, have realized that their unique music and message needed to be copyrighted, and trademarked in order to protect their music and their names. As a matter of fact, many Black composers and artists allege that their un-copyrighted work was stolen, but some Black composers and musicians did purchase trademarks.

---

[7] Samuel Floyd Jr., The Power of Black Music Interpreting It's History From Africa to the United States, 1995, page 5.
[8] Ra Un Nefer Amen, Metu Neter Volume I, 1990

Name City, State, Country	Trademark Names:	Trademarks Live or Dead
Chuck Berry™ St. Louis, Missouri	Johnny B. Goode; Hail! Hail ! Rock n' Roll	Four
Fisk Jubilee Singers™ Nashville, Tennessee	Fisk Jubilee Singers; Fisk University Jubilee Singers; Jubilee Singers; Fisk University, Nashville, Tenn. Incorporated, Aug. 24, 1867 Jubilee Singers	Six
Count Basie Red Bank, New Jersey	Count Basie Orchestra	Two
Cab Calloway™ Rochester, New York	The Cab Calloway Orchestra; Cab Calloway	Two
Miles Davis™ Alton, Illinois	Miles Davis; Miles	Three
Duke Ellington™ Washington, DC.	The Duke Ellington Orchestra; Duke Ellington	Six
Five Blind Boy's of Alabama,Talladega, Alabama	Five Blind Boys of Alabama; The Original Five Blind Boys of Alabama	Two
Dizzy Gillespie Cheraw, South Carolina	Dizzy Gillespie	Two
Wynton Marsalis New Orleans, Louisiana	Marsalis Music, Anything is Possible, Crescent City Communications	Two

Many other influential Black artists have no trademarks, even though their music and compositions are world known. Miriam Makeba, "Mama Afrika" of Johannesburg, South Africa, and "Ladysmith Black Mambazo of KwaZulu-Natal, South Africa, have both won Grammys although their work has not been trademarked.

Africans in the Diaspora have created blues, jazz, spirituals, calypso, soca, bebop, scat, rhythm and blues, soul, reggae, hip-hop, mambo and rap. These lucrative musical forms are rooted in the Black experience from Africa, the Americas, and the Caribbean.

The following recording artists and groups have trademarked their recording names and or groups. Newer music genres such as jazz, hip-hop, rap, reggae and calypso, have also been trademarked.

[148]

Otis Blackwell, of Brooklyn, New York, had a very successful run as a prolific songwriter. He wrote nearly one thousand songs, including those written under his alias John Davenport. His legacy includes a number of top-selling rock-and-roll records such as: Fever, Don't Be Cruel, All Shook Up, One Broken Heart For Sale, Return To Sender, Hey Little Girl, Breathless, Great Balls Of Fire, Easy Question, Handyman, Hello Bottle, Sleep Is Just Around the Corner, and Clinging to a Dream.

James Brown™, Barnwell, South Carolina, has two trademarks, the Godfather of Soul™, and Soul Brother Number One™. A man whose early childhood was full of trouble and strife. James Brown faced a variety of obstacles. In spite of his trials, he became a mentor and an inspirational example in his lifetime. Always proud to be a Black man, Mr. Brown turned out hits such as Please, Please, Please, Say it Loud, I'm Black and Proud, Poppa Got a Brand New Bag, to just name a few. Mr. Brown was a businessman, innovator and genius, who never forgot where he came from. His ingenuity will be missed, but never forgotten.

Sean "P. Diddy" Combs™, New York, New York, with forty-four trademarks has expanded his music career into fashion and other business ventures. His hit songs include Every Breath You Take, and Missing You. There are forty-four trademarks attached to the Sean Jean name. In addition, Mr. Combs' "Making the Band 2, 3 and 4" is changing the means of discovering and developing new talent.

Celia Cruz™, Havana, Cuba, has two trademarks, was a three time Grammy Award winner and a four time Latin Grammy Award winner. Ms. Cruz was an Afro-Cuban woman who put salsa on the world stage with songs such as Tu Voz, Burundanga, and Cao Cao Mani Picao.

Grandmaster Flash™ (Joseph Saddler), Bridgetown, Barbados, has four trademarks. DJ Kool Herc™ (Clive Campbell), Kingston, Jamaica, owns one trademark, Afrika Bambaataa & the Soul Sonic Force™ owns one trademark and a host of other DJ's, rappers and musicians have forever left their mark on the music world and Hip Hop. Hip Hop is a multi-billion dollar a year industry, and there are now over one thousand trademarks that are associated with the term Hip-Hop.

[149]

B. B King™, Itta Bena, Mississippi, is known as the King of Blues. Mr. King's mastery of the guitar has electrified and thrilled audiences for over fifty years. With hits such as Three O'clock Blues, Paying The Cost To Be The Boss (1968) and The Thrill Is Gone, B. B. King has won thirteen Grammys and countless awards.

Jimi Hendrix™, Seattle, Washington, mastered the electric guitar and revolutionized rock and roll and the art of live performance. He is noted for the popular songs – Are You Experienced and Purple Haze. Although he has been dead for over thirty years, his popularity keeps growing, as does the number of trademarks attached to his name. There are now seventy-four trademarks attached to the name, Jimi Hendrix.

Whitney Houston™, Newark, New Jersey, a pop diva, whose commanding voice, has captured audiences everywhere, has many popular songs, including: Saving All My Love For You, I Wanna Dance With Somebody, I Will Always Love You, and others. There are six trademarks associated with Whitney Houston's name.

Quincy D. Jones, Jr.™, Chicago, Illinois, conductor, record producer, musical arranger, film composer and trumpeter, has had seventy Grammy Award nominations and has won twenty-five. In 1991, Quincy Jones earned the Grammy Legends Award. He produced two of the top-selling records of all time, Thriller (Michael Jackson) and We Are the World, which generated large charitable donations. He has also performed a number of solo songs including: Walking in Space, You've Got It Bad, Girl, Body Heat, and Mellow Madness. He has also arranged songs for Frank Sinatra, Ella Fitzgerald, Peggy Lee and Dinah Washington. In addition, Quincy Jones has composed musical scores for over thirty major films and three television shows and owns over thirty trademarks.

Solomon Popoli Linda, South Africa, a Zulu migrant worker, composed The Lion Sleeps Tonight. His family is currently suing Disney for royalties. Mr. Solomon Linda died in poverty in 1962. In 1939, he first recorded the song under the title "Mbube", Zulu for "the Lion". Linda was only paid ten shillings for the song; it went on to sell 100,000 copies. Pete Seeger, an American folk

[150]

singer, re-recorded the song under the name "Wimoweh". In 1951, Seeger's band, the Weavers copied the song "note for note" and sold more than one million copies. In 1961, when a recording by the Weavers transformed the song into The Lion Sleeps Tonight, the song reached the top of the hit parade eight times and has been played on American radio for over thirty years. In 1994, Disney's production of "The Lion King" propelled this song to another round of world-wide popularity. Since the song's original writing, the Solomon Linda estate has received only $15,000 in royalties.

Bob Marley™, St. Ann Parish, Jamaica, West Indies. Mr. Marley's songwriting, singing, guitar playing and lyrics revolutionized reggae and empowered people of color and others who appreciated his lyrics. His songs are forever etched in the psyche of millions of people. I Shot the Sheriff, Get up, Stand up, Buffalo Soldier, and Africa Unite, are a few of the many popular songs. that Bob Marley has written and performed. Nine trademarks are associated with Bob Marley's name.

"Ray Charles" Robinson™, Albany, Georgia, a self-made millionaire, High Priest of Soul and inventor of modern soul music. Ray Charles' innovation and crossover appeal made him a mega star on the world stage. Some hits include: I Can't Stop Loving You, Hit The Road Jack, I Chose To Sing The Blues, Georgia on Mind, and Unchain My Heart. These songs written by a blind, Black man, characterize an unforgettable era in American music. Mr. Charles was a musical genius who did not let his lack of sight deter him. His life story was recently made into a feature length film. Jamie Foxx, the actor who portrayed Mr. Charles, won an Academy Award.

Russell Simmons™, Queens, New York, a businessman, entrepreneur, and great humanitarian. Mr. Simmons, over the years, has become a multi-millionaire. The focus of his life is now to bring about social change; through empowerment, he generously assists those in need. Mr. Simmons is one of the leading forces behind Rush Communications™ (one hundred fifteen trademarks), Russell Simmons Music Group and Def Jam (over one hundred trademarks). He also founded Phat Farm (over fifty trademarks).

[151]

The list above represents only a small sample of artists who have transformed music into the sounds that are downloaded, purchased and otherwise sought after globally. These artists, entertainers and entrepreneurs have come to realize that their names and music should be protected through trademarks and copyrights.

Where Does the Black Inventor Stand Today?

Black inventors have shaped and continue to influence the world today. A number of inventors have established their own companies and corporations and use their ideas to generate income for themselves, their families and their communities. More research needs to be done on the impact of Black innovators and inventors on the development of world economies. Globally, corporations continue to benefit from the innovations, inventions and ideas of Black inventors. Below is a list of companies that own patents filed by Black inventors.

Name of Inventors	Company patents are assigned to	Total Number of Patents
Thedros W. Mariam, Emmanuel Kwaku Ankutse, Uzodinma Okoranyanu, Effiong Ibok	Advanced Micro Devices, Inc., Sunnyvale, CA.	Seventy-six
Jesse E. Russell, Nathaniel R. Quick, James E. West, Charles O. Akanbi, Yaw Obeng, James W. Mitchell	AT&T Corporation, AT&T Bell Corporation	One hundred ninety five patents
Thomas O. Mensah, Lynn O. Okorocha, George Y. Adusei, Dr. Carlton M. Truesdale, Diana M. Young, et al.	Corning Glass Works, Corning Inc., Corning Precision Lens	Fifty seven
Sama N. Hyacinth, George Anim-Ansah, Femi Ayoola	British Telecommunication Public Limited Co., United Kingdom	Seven
Helen Mawudeku, Rotimi Aluk	Canada Natural Resources, Canada	two
Tidjani Bouchami, Mamadou Daffe, Ali Kone, Fred K. Kanamplu	Centre National de la Recherche Scientifique(CSNR), France	Six
Sape K. Quashie, Dotsevi Y. Sogah, Wendell W. Wilkerson, Kofi S. Amuti, et al.	E.I. du Pont de Nemours and Company, Delaware	Ninety
John E. Bradley, Oludele O Popoola, Edward Akpan, Samuel A. Gebremariam, Michael G. Ellis, Patricia B. Reid, Allen H. Turner, et al.	Ford Global Technologies, Ford Motor Company, Michigan	Eighty-one
Marshall G. Jones, James H. Logan, Granville T. Woods, Yaw D.	General Electric, Schenectady, New York	One hundred fifty

[153]

Yeboah, Gilbert Farmer, John Y. Ofori, et al.		
Joseph Gamell	Joseph Gamell Industries, Michigan	Fourteen
Marc E. Dean, Ajamu A. Wesley, Eskinder Hailu, Cyrian E. Uzoh, Ernest L. Walker, Jody B. Joyner, Sandra J. Baylor et al.	International Business Machine, Armonk, NY.	Two hundred forty-five
Lonnie G. Johnson	Johnson Research and Development, Georgia	Sixty-eight
Dr. Percy L. Julian	Julian Laboratories, Illinois	Ten
Abolade Gbadegsin, Oshoma Momoh, Keith M. Toussaint et al.	Microsoft Corporation, Redmond, Washington	Thirty-four
Robert K. Mensah, Kwodwo Ofori, Kingley Opoku-Gyamfi	Commonwealth Scientific and Industrial Research Organization, Orange, Australia	Four Patents
Ndungu Kariku	Kari – Tyrpanosomiasis Research Center, Kikuyu, Kenya	One
Kubuta, Bruno Kilunga	Osaka Bioscience Institute, Suita-shi, Japan	One
Benjamin F. Johnson	Stark Engineering and Research, Monrovia, Liberia	Two
Philippe Rasoanaivo, et al.	Institut Malagache De Recherches Appliqués, Antananarivo, Madagascar and Rhone-Poulenc Rorer, S.A., Anthony, France	Two
Salime Sylla, et al.	Hydro Quebec (Canada); Centre Nat Research Scient (France)	Six
Kenneth R Scott	Howard University, Washington, DC.	Eight
Samuel Dixon, Jr.	U.S. Army, Washington, DC.	Twenty
Charles Wambebe, et. al.	National Institute for Pharmaceutical Research, Nigeria	Six
Abdou M. Dioffo	State of Niger represented by the Minister of Public Labour (buildings, bridges, roads, highways)	Two

Table 38: List of Black inventors and companies (patents assigned to)

In this short book, I have sought to give enough information about Black innovators and inventors, so that no matter where we are in the world we will see how our lives have been enriched and influenced by the inventions, innovations and trademarks of Black men and women. This book also highlights the global scope of Black inventors and their inventions. The international impact of Black inventors will be further explored in my upcoming book: *Black Innovators and Inventors and Their Impact on Global Economies, Volume I.* For additional information on Black and indigenous innovators and inventors please contact:

Global Black Inventor Research Projects, Inc.

Email: info@globalblackinventor.com or kcholmes50@gmail.com

Bibliography and Works Cited

UK Intellectual Property Office. esp@cenet Home Page. 2008. 2006 йил 06-Jan 2007 <http://gb.espacenet.com>.

Wikipedia Foundations, Inc. Black People. 2008 йил 01-June . 2008 йил 20-June <http://en.wikipedia.org/wiki/Black_people>.

White, Lorraine. The History of Blacks in Britain. 1994 йил Sep. 2008 йил 31-May <http://www.socialistalternative.org/literature/panther/ch4.html>.

African Studies Center, Boston University developed by Johnston, Deborah Smith and Brown, Barbara. "Mollweide Equal Area Project." 1998. Outreach Progam African Studies Center, Boston University. 2007 йил Nov <www.bu.edu/africa/outreach>.

Amin, Samir. "Africa in world mining geography." 1988 йил - . 2008 йил 29-March <http://www.unu.edu/unupress/unupbooks/uu29me/uu29me05.htm>.

—. Africa in world mining geography. 1988. 2008 йил 29-March <http://www.unu.edu/unupress/unupbooks/uu29me/uu29me05.htm>.

Black Latin America. 2002. 2007 йил 31-May <http://whgbetc.com/mind/black-latin-america2.html>.

Ezeh, Chris. "Introduction to facts on Africa." 2008. EuroAfricalCentral Online Magazine - http://www.eac-magazine.com. 2008 йил 29-March <http://www.eac-magazine.com/en/index.php?option=com_content&task=view&id=13&Itemid=29>.

Faostat.fao.org. Nations, Food and Agricultural Organization of the United Nations. 2005. 2008 йил 31-May <www.faostat.fao.org>.

Floyd, Jr., Samuel A. "Introduction." Floyd, Jr. Samuel A. The Power of Black Music, Interpreting It's History From Africa to The United States. New York, NY.: Oxford University Press, 1995. 5.

Google. Google Patent Search. 2008. 2007 йил 06-Jan <http://www.google.com/patents>.

NationMaster.com. Agriculture Statistics - Arable and permanent cropland (most recent) by country. 2000. 2007 йил 31-Dec. <http://www.nationmaster.com/graph/agr_ara_and_per_cro-agriculture-arable-and-permanent-cropland>.

—. Agriculture Statistics - Banana production (most recent) by country. 2000. 2007 йил 31-Dec. <http://www.nationmaster.com/graph/agr_ban_pro-agriculture-banana-production>.

—. Agriculture Statistics - Cereal production (most recent) by country. 1999-2001. 2007 йил 31-Dec. <http://www.nationmaster.com/graph/agr_cer_pro-agriculture-cereal-production>.

—. Agriculture Statistics - Cereal production (most recent) by Country. 2003/2004. 2008 йил 28-March <http://www.nationmaster.com/graph/agr_cer_pro-agriculture-cereal-production>.

—. Agriculture Statistics - Cotton production (most recent) by country. 2003/2004. 2007 йил 31-Dec. <http://www.nationmaster.com/graph/agr_cot_pro-agriculture-cotton-production>.

—. Agriculture Statistics - Peanut production (most recent) by country. 2003/2004. 2007 йил 31-Dec <http://www.nationmaster.com/graph/agr_pro_pea-agriculture-production-peanut>.

—. Agriculture Statistics - Peanut production (most recent) by country. 2003/2004. 2008 йил 29-March <http://www.nationmaster.com/graph/agr_pro_pea-agriculture-production-peanut/AFR>.

—. Agriculture Statistics - Soybean production (most recent) by country. 2003-2004. 2008 йил 29-March <http://www.nationmaster.com/graph/agr_pro_soy-agriculture-production-soybean/AFR>.

—. Agriculture Statistics - Soybean production, (most recent) by country. 2003/2004. 2008 йил 31-May <http://www.nationmaster.com/graph/agr_pro_soy-agriculture-production-soybean>.

—. Agriculture Statistics - Sorghum production (most recent) by country. 2003/2004. 2007 йил 31-Dec <http://www.nationmaster.com/graph/agr_pro_sor-agriculture-production-sorghum>.

—. Patents Granted per million people 1998. 1998. 2007 йил 29-Mar <www.nationmaster.com/graph/eco_pat_gr-economy-patents-granted/AFR>.

Mutume, Gumisai. http://www.un.org/ecosocdev/geninfo/afrec/vol17no2/172brain.htm. 2003 йил July. 2008 йил 31-May <www.africarcovery.org>.

Mannix, Daniel A. and Cowley, Malcolm. "The Beginnings." Mannix, Daniel A. and Cowley, Malcolm. Black Cargoes, A History of the Atlantic Slave Trade. New York: Viking Press, 1962. 11.

Merriam . "Websters Third New International Dictionary of the English Lanuage Unabridged." Staff, Philip Babock Gove and The Mieriam Editorial. Websters Third New International Dictionary of the English Lanuage Unabridged. Springfield: Meriam-Webster Inc.., 1986. 188.

Office-gb.espacenet.com, European Patent. Advanced Search - European Patent Office. 2008. 2008 йил 29-March <http://ep.espacenet.com>.

"Websters Third New International Dictionary of the English Lanuage Unabridged." Philip Babcock Gove, Editor in Chief. Websters Third New International Dictionary of the English Lanuage Unabridged. Springfield, MA.: Merriam-Webster Publsiher, 1986. 1654.

Rodney, Walter. "How Europe Became the Dominant Section of a World-Wide Trade System." Rodney, Walter. How Europe Underdeveloped Africa. Washington, DC.: Howard University Press, 1982. 80.

Rodney, Walter. "Technical Stagnation and Distortion of the African Economy in the Pre-Colonial Epoch." Rodney, Walter. How Europe Underdeveloped Africa. Washington, DC.: Howard University Press, 1982. 106.

[157]

The Generations Network. www.ancestry.com. 2007. 2007 йил 29-Mar
<www.ancestry.com>.

Recommended Reading List

Baker, Henry E. *The Colored Inventor: A Record of Fifty Years,* New York: Crisis Publishing Company, 1913.

Becoat, Bill. *Dream Peddler: The Story of an Entrepreneur,* St. Louis, Mo: Fokl P Power Publishers, 1995.

McKinley, Jr., Burt *Black Inventor of America.* Portland, Oregon: National Book Company, 1989.

Dingle, Derek T. *Black Enterprises Titans of the B.E. 100's Black CEO's Who Redefined and Conquered American Business,* John Wiley & Sons, Inc., New York, 1999.

Durham, Philip and Jones, Everett L. *The Negro Cowboys,* Cornwall, New York, 1965.

Gilbert, Erik and Reynolds Johnathan T. *Africa in World History From Prehistory to the Present, Pearson Education,* Upper Saddle River, New Jersey, 2004.

Haber, Louis. *Black Pioneers of Science and Invention.* New York: Harcourt, Brace & World, 1970.

James, Portia P. *The Real McCoy African-American Invention and Innovation,* 1619-1930, Washington, D.C., Anacostia Museum of the Smithsonian Institution, 1989.

Lucas, A. and Harris, J.R. *Ancient Egyptian Materials and Industries,* Mineola Publications, Inc., 1999.

Makinde, Bankole. *Who's Who in Nigeria 2nd Edition,* Newswatch Book Limited, Lagos State, Nigeria, 2001.

Ott, Virginia and Swanson, Gloria. *Man with a Million Ideas, Fred Jones Genius/Inventor,* Lerner Publication Company, Minneapolis, Minnesota, 1977.

Rodney, Walter. *How Europe Underdeveloped Africa,* Bogle-L'Overture Publications, London and Tanzanian Publishing House, Dar es Salaam, Tanzania

Sammons Vivian O. *Black in Science and Medicine,* New York, Hemisphere Publishing Company, 1990.

Sluby, Patricia Carter. *The Inventive Spirit of African Americans, Patented Ingenuity,* Westport, Connecticut, Praeger Publishers, 2004.

Turner III, Morris. *America's Black Towns and Settlements, A Historical Reference Guide, Volume I.* Missing Pages Production, Rohnert Park, California, 1998.

Walker, Juliet E.K. *The History of Black Business in America: Capitalism, Race Entrepreneurship,* Twayne Publishers, 1998.

Warren, Wini. *Black Women Scientists in the United States,* Indiana University Press, Bloomington, Indiana, 1999.

Webster, Raymond B. *African American Firsts in Science and Technology,* Gale Group, Detroit, Michigan, 1999.

Woodson, Carter G. and Wesley, Charles H. *Negro Makers of History 5th Edition Revised,* Washington, D.C., The Associated Publishers, Inc. 1958.

Mannix, Dennis P. and Cowley, Malcolm. *Black Cargoes, A History of the Atlantic Slave Trade, 1518-1865,* New York, The Viking Press, 1962.

Index

[162]

[169]

McCoy, Elijah
  Colchester, Ontario, Canada, over forty seven
    patents, 15
  Detroit, MI., 1872-1923., 74
  inducted in National Inventors Hall of Fame,
    2001, 56
  patented lubricating devices for machinery,
    trains, ships, 52
McGee, Hansel
  Bronx, NY., 1964-65, 78
Mchuma, Frank S.
  Dar-Es-Salaam, Tanzania, 1983, 39
Mckie, Derrick B.
  Brooklyn, NY., 1986-2001, 78
McNabb, Donavan
  Chicago, IL., two trademarks, 143
McNair, Steve
  Mount Olive, MS., four trademarks, 144
McNeil, Vincent M.
  Dallas, TX., 1998-2002, 83
Medley, Clarence
  Alberta, Canada, 1907, 112
Mekuria, Dr. Fisseha
  Lund, Sweden, 2000-2006, 126
Mendenhall, Albert
  Oskaloosa, IA., 1899-1925, 70
Mensah, Robert Kofi
  New South Wales, Australia, 1997-2003, 110
Mensah, Thomas
  Noscross, GA., 1988-1995, 69
Mensah, Timmi
  Kobenhavn, Denmark, 1997, 124
Merkuria, Dr. Fisseha
  Sweden, 2000-2006, 123
Microsoft Corporation, Redmond, Washington
  Black inventors filed for thirty-four patents,
    154
Miles, Alexander
  Duluth, Minnesota, 1883, 38
  inducted into National Inventors Hall of Fame,
    2007, 56
Miley, George H.
  Champaign, IL., 1975-2001, 69
Military records
  Civil War Soldiers, identify Black troops as
    Colored, 25
Miller, Buddie
  Trinidad & Tobago, 2004-2008, 117
Mitchell, Roger E.
  Bloomington, MN. 1997-1999, 74
Mock, James R.
  Elizabethtown, Kentucky, 1859, 37
Momoh, Oshoma
  Sierra Leone, 1999-2002, 105

Montgomery, Peter T.
  Mound Bayou, MS., 1892, 75
Moore, Emmanuel M.
  Pine Bluff, AR., 1958-1970, 64
Moore, Roy J.
  Columbia, SC., 1986-1996, 83
Moore, Samuel
  Cleveland, OH., 1928-1935, 80
  Fairmont, W.VA., 1926-1927, 86
Morgan, Garrett Augustus
  inducted into National Inventors Hall of Fame,
    2005, 56
Morris, Morgan H.
  Schenectady, NY., 1982-1993, 79
Mosby, Frederick A.
  Shaker Heights, OH., 1961-1970, 81
Moses, John R
  Annapolis, MD., 1981-2001, 71
Moses, Robert P.
  Cambridge, MA., 1996, 72
Mossi, Boureima
  Niamy, Niger, 38
Mukena, Mulongo M.
  Lurunbashi, Shaba, Zaire, 1988, 40
Murray, George
  Alexandria, Virginia, 1870, 40
Murray, George W.
  Rempert, SC., fourteen patents, 15
  Sumter, SC., 1894-1908, 83
Mutabingwa, Theonest K.
  Muheza, Tanzania, 2007, 105
Mwanika, Christine Mayambala-
  Mishawaka, IN., 1986, 94
Nacoulma, Odile G.
  Ouagaougou, Burkina Faso, 2004, 101
Napier, Dennis K.
  Sacramento, CA., 1992, 66
Nare, Christine
  Ouagadougou, Burkina Faso, 92
Nascimento, Edson Arantes do (Pele)
  Tres Coracoes, Brazil, seventeen trademarks,
    143
National Institute for Pharmaceutical Research,
    Nigeria
  Black inventors filed for six patents, 154
Native American
  Inventors, 1888-1995, 89
Ndagijimana, Robin
  Neuss, Germany, 2004, 94
Ndiaye, Baila
  Santa Clara, CA., 2003, 66
Ndlovu, Carol V.
  Capetown, South Africa, 1992, 94, 105
Ndong, Andres Michi

[172]

[175]

[177]

About The Author

Keith Holmes was born in Queens, New York and currently lives with his family in Brooklyn. He has published in:
The New York Observer, June 1992,
The Black World Today, Feb 2002,
AfricanAmerica.org, 2008,
AfricaFiles.org, 2007,
Africapath.com, 2007,
Afrigeneas.com, 2007,
Africaresource.com, 2008,
AllAfrica.com
Barbados Free Press, 2007,
Black-history-month.co.uk, 2007,
BlackNews.com, 2008,
Island Sun Newspaper, 2008,
Jamaicans.com, 2007,
Louisiana Weekly, 2008,
MyAfricanDiaspora.com, 2007,
Pambazuka.org, 2007,

For twenty-four years, Mr. Holmes has worked in the satellite communications industry, and since 1977, he has used computers from main frames to personal computers. Mr. Holmes has spent considerable time researching information on Black inventors at the New York Patent Library, the Schomburg Library in New York and the Howard University's Moorland-Spingarn Research Center in Washington, DC. He has lectured in California, Connecticut, Illinois, New York, New Jersey, North Carolina, Pennsylvania, Virginia and Washington, DC, and is currently working on several projects about Black inventors. Mr. Holmes has spent twenty years researching information on Black innovators and inventors from around the world.

For additional copies of *Black Inventors, Crafting Over 200 Years of Success*

Call: 646-610-1485 or send a check or money order for:
$15.00 (plus shipping and handling United States orders). For Canadian and international orders please contact:

Global Black Inventor Research Projects, Inc.
1023 Beverley Road
Brooklyn, New York 11218.
Website: www.globalblackinventor.com
Email: info@globalblackinventor.com or
kcholmes50@gmail.com

Facebook: Global Black Inventor Research Projects, Inc.
Twitter: Globalblkinvtr
Linkedin: Keith Holmes

CPSIA information can be obtained at www.ICGtesting.com
Printed in the USA
BVOW020414150713

325817BV00003BA/4/P

9 780979 957307